*What
Makes You
Not a Buddhist*

What
Makes You
Not a Buddhist

Dzongsar Jamyang Khyentse

Shambhala
Boston & London
2007

Shambhala Publications, Inc.
Horticultural Hall
300 Massachusetts Avenue
Boston, Massachusetts 02115
www.shambhala.com

9 8 7 6 5 4 3 2

Printed in the United States of America

⊗This edition is printed on acid-free paper that meets the
American National Standards Institute z39.48 Standard.
Distributed in the United States by Random House, Inc.,
and in Canada by Random House of Canada Ltd

Design by Dede Cummings & Carolyn Kasper / DCDESIGN

Library of Congress Cataloging-in-Publication Data
Dzongshar Jamyang Khyentse, Rinpoche.
What makes you not a Buddhist/Dzongsar Jamyang
Khyentse.   ɪ
p. cm.
ISBN-13: 978-1-59030-406-8 (hardcover: alk. paper)
ISBN-10: 1-59030-406-3
1. Buddhism—Doctrines. I. Title.
BQ4132.D96 2007
294.3'42—dc22
2006021536

For the son of Suddhodana, the prince of India,
Without whom I would still not know I am a wanderer

Contents

What
Makes You
Not a Buddhist

Introduction

Once, I was seated on a plane in the middle seat of the middle row on a trans-Atlantic flight, and the sympathetic man sitting next to me made an attempt to be friendly. Seeing my shaved head and maroon skirt, he gathered that I was a Buddhist. When the meal was served, the man considerately offered to order a vegetarian meal for me. Having correctly assumed that I was a Buddhist, he also assumed that I don't eat meat. That was the beginning of our chat. The flight was long, so to kill our boredom, we discussed Buddhism.

Over time I have come to realize that people often associate Buddhism and Buddhists with peace, meditation, and nonviolence. In fact many seem to think that saffron or maroon robes and a peaceful smile are all it takes to be a Buddhist. As a fanatical Buddhist myself, I must take pride in this reputation, particularly the nonviolent aspect of it, which is so rare in this age of war and violence, and especially religious violence. Throughout the history of humankind, religion seems to beget brutality. Even today religious-extremist violence dominates the news. Yet I think I can say with confidence that so far we Buddhists have not disgraced ourselves. Violence has never played a part in propagating Buddhism. However, as a trained Buddhist, I also feel a little discontented when Buddhism is associated with nothing beyond vegetarianism, nonviolence, peace, and meditation. Prince Siddhartha, who sacrificed all the comforts and luxuries of palace life, must have been searching for more than passivity and shrubbery when he set out to discover enlightenment.

Although essentially very simple, Buddhism cannot be easily explained. It is almost inconceivably complex, vast, and deep. Although it is nonreligious and nontheistic, it's difficult to present Buddhism without sounding theoretical and religious. As Buddhism traveled to different parts of the world, the cultural characteristics it accumulated have made it even more complicated to decipher. Theistic trappings such as incense, bells, and multicolored hats can attract people's attention, but at the same time they can be obstacles. People end up thinking that is all there is to Buddhism and are diverted from its essence.

Sometimes out of frustration that Siddhartha's teachings have not caught on enough for my liking, and sometimes out of my own ambition, I entertain ideas of reforming Buddhism, making it easier—more straightforward and puritanical. It is devious and misguided to imagine (as I sometimes do) simplifying Buddhism into defined, calculated practices like meditating three times a day, adhering to certain dress codes, and holding certain ideological beliefs, such as that the whole world must be converted to Buddhism. If we could promise that such practices would provide immediate, tangible results, I think there would be more Buddhists in the world. But when I recover from these fantasies (which I rarely do), my sober mind warns me that a world of people calling themselves Buddhists would not necessarily be a better world.

Many people mistakenly think that Buddha is the "God" of Buddhism; even some people in commonly recognized Buddhist countries such as Korea, Japan, and Bhutan have this theistic approach to the Buddha and Buddhism. This is why throughout this book we use the name Siddhartha and Buddha interchangeably, to remind people that Buddha was just a man and that this man became Buddha.

It is understandable that some people might think that Buddhists are followers of this external man named Buddha. However, Buddha himself pointed out that we should not venerate a person but rather the wisdom that person teaches. Similarly, it is taken for granted that reincarnation and karma are the most essential beliefs of Buddhism. There are numerous other gross misconceptions. For example, Tibetan Buddhism is sometimes referred to as "lamaism," and Zen is not even considered Buddhism in some cases. Those people who are slightly more informed, yet still misguided, may use words such as *emptiness* and *nirvana* without understanding their meaning.

When a conversation arises like the one with my seatmate on the plane, a non-Buddhist may casually ask, "What makes someone a Buddhist?" That is the hardest question to answer. If the person has a genuine interest, the complete answer does not make for light dinner conversation, and generalizations can lead to misunderstanding. Suppose that you give them the true answer, the answer that points to the very foundation of this 2,500-year-old tradition.

One is a Buddhist if he or she accepts the following four truths:

All compounded things are impermanent.
All emotions are pain.
All things have no inherent existence.
Nirvana is beyond concepts.

These four statements, spoken by the Buddha himself, are known as "the four seals." Traditionally, *seal* means something like a hallmark that confirms authenticity. For the sake of simplicity and flow we will refer to these statements herein as both seals and "truths," not to be confused with Buddhism's four noble truths, which pertain solely to aspects of suffering. Even though the four seals are believed to encompass all of Buddhism, people don't seem to want to hear about them. Without further explanation they serve only to dampen spirits and fail to inspire further interest in many cases. The topic of conversation changes and that's the end of it.

The message of the four seals is meant to be understood literally, not metaphorically or mystically—and meant to be taken seriously. But the seals are not edicts or commandments. With a little contemplation one sees that there is nothing moralistic or ritualistic about them. There is no mention of good or bad behavior. They are secular truths based on wisdom, and wisdom is the primary concern of a Buddhist. Morals and ethics are secondary. A few puffs of a cigarette and a little fooling around don't prevent someone from becoming a Buddhist. That is not to say that we have license to be wicked or immoral.

Broadly speaking, wisdom comes from a mind that has what the Buddhists call "right view." But one doesn't even have to consider oneself a Buddhist to have right view. Ultimately it is this view that determines our motivation and action. It is the view that guides us on the path of Buddhism. If we can adopt wholesome behaviors in addition to the four seals, it makes us even better Buddhists. But what makes you not a Buddhist?

If you cannot accept that all compounded or fabricated things are impermanent, if you believe that there is some essential substance or concept that is permanent, then you are not a Buddhist.

If you cannot accept that all emotions are pain, if you believe that actually some emotions are purely pleasurable, then you are not a Buddhist.

If you cannot accept that all phenomena are illusory and empty, if you believe that certain things do exist inherently, then you are not a Buddhist.

And if you think that enlightenment exists within the spheres of time, space, and power, then you are not a Buddhist.

So, what makes you a Buddhist? You may not have been born in a Buddhist country or to a Buddhist family, you may not wear robes or shave your head, you may eat meat and idolize Eminem and Paris Hilton. That doesn't mean you cannot be a Buddhist. In order to be a Buddhist, you must accept that all compounded phenomena are impermanent, all emotions are pain, all things have no inherent existence, and enlightenment is beyond concepts.

It's not necessary to be constantly and endlessly mindful of these four truths. But they must reside in your mind. You don't walk around persistently remembering your own name, but when someone asks your name, you remember it instantly. There is no doubt. Anyone who accepts these four seals, even independently of Buddha's teachings, even never having heard the name Shakyamuni Buddha, can be considered to be on the same path as he.

When I tried to explain all of this to the man next to me on the plane, I began to hear a soft snoring sound and realized that he was sound asleep. Apparently our conversation did not kill his boredom.

I enjoy generalizing, and as you read this book, you will find a sea of generalizations. But I justify this to myself by thinking that apart from generalizations we human beings don't have much means of communication. That's a generalization in itself.

By writing this book, it is not my aim to persuade people to follow Shakyamuni Buddha, become Buddhists, and practice the dharma. I deliberately do not mention any meditation techniques, practices, or mantras. My primary intention is to point out the unique part of Buddhism that differentiates it from other views. What did this Indian prince say that earned so much respect and admiration, even from skeptical modern scientists like Albert Einstein? What did he say that moved thousands of pilgrims to prostrate themselves all the way from Tibet to Bodh Gaya? What sets Buddhism apart from the religions of the world? I believe it boils down to the four seals, and I have attempted to present these difficult concepts in the simplest language available to me.

Siddhartha's priority was to get down to the root of the problem. Buddhism is not culturally bound. Its benefits are not limited to any particular society and have no place in government and politics. Siddhartha was not interested in academic treatises and scientifically provable theories. Whether the world is flat or round did not concern him. He had a different kind of practicality. He wanted to get to the bottom of suffering. I hope to illustrate that his teachings are not a grandiose intellectual philosophy to be read and then shelved, but a functional, logical view that can be practiced by each and every individual. To that end I have attempted to use examples from all aspects of all walks of life—from the romantic crush to the emergence of civilization as we know it. While these examples are different from the ones Siddhartha used, the same message Siddhartha expressed is still relevant today.

But Siddhartha also said that his words should not be taken for granted without analysis. So, definitely someone as ordinary as myself must also be scrutinized, and I invite you to analyze what you find within these pages.

one

Fabrication and Impermanence

*B*uddha *was not a celestial being. He was a simple* human. But not too simple, for he was a prince. He went by the name Siddhartha Gautama, and he enjoyed a privileged life— a beautiful palace in Kapilavastu, a loving wife and son, adoring parents, loyal subjects, lush gardens with peacocks, and a host of well-endowed courtesans. His father, Suddhodana, made sure that his every need was taken care of and his every wish fulfilled within the palace walls. For when Siddhartha was a baby, an astrologer had predicted that the prince might choose to become a hermit in his later life, and Suddhodana was determined that Siddhartha would succeed him as king. Palace life was luxurious, sheltered, and also quite peaceful. Siddhartha never quarreled with his family; in fact, he cared for them and loved them very much. He had easy relations with everyone, apart from occasional tension with one of his cousins.

As Siddhartha grew older, he became curious about his country and the world beyond. Bending to his son's pleas, the king agreed to let the prince venture beyond the palace walls on an excursion, but he gave strict instructions to the chariot driver, Channa, that the prince should be exposed only to things beautiful and wholesome. Indeed, Siddhartha very much enjoyed the mountains and the rivers and all the natural wealth of this earth. But on the way home, the two came upon a peasant who was groaning by the roadside, wracked with pain from some excruciating illness. All his life Siddhartha had been surrounded by strapping body guards and healthy ladies of the court; the sound of groans and the sight of a disease-wracked body were shocking to him. Witnessing the vulnerability of the human body impressed him deeply, and he returned to the palace with a heavy heart.

As time passed, the prince seemingly returned to normal, but he longed to make another journey. Again Suddhodana reluctantly agreed. This time Siddhartha saw a toothless old crone hobbling along, and he immediately ordered Channa to stop.

He asked his driver, "Why is this person walking so?"

"She's old, my lord," said Channa.

"What is 'old'?" asked Siddhartha.

"The elements of her body have been used and worn out over a long time," said Channa. Shaken by this spectacle, Siddhartha let Channa drive him home.

Now Siddhartha's curiosity could not be abated—what else was out there? So off he and Channa went on a third journey. Again he enjoyed the beauty of the region, the mountains and the streams. But as they were returning home, they came upon four pallbearers carrying a flat, lifeless body on a palanquin. Siddhartha had never in his life seen such a thing. Channa explained that the frail body was actually dead.

Siddhartha asked, "Will death come to others?"

Channa answered, "Yes, my lord, it will come to all."

"To my father? Even to my son?"

"Yes, to everyone. Whether you are rich or poor, high caste or low, you cannot escape death. It is the fate of all who are born on this earth."

Upon first hearing the story of the dawn of Siddhartha's realization, we might think that he was remarkably unsophisticated.

It seems strange to hear of a prince, raised to lead an entire king-dom, asking such simplistic questions. But *we* are the ones who are naive. In this information age we are surrounded by images of decay and death—beheadings, bullfights, bloody murder. Far from reminding us of our own fate, these images are used for entertainment and profit. Death has become a consumer prod-uct. Most of us do not contemplate the nature of death on a deep level. We don't acknowledge that our bodies and environment are made up of unstable elements that can fall apart with even the slightest provocation. Of course we know that one day we will die. But most of us, unless we have been diagnosed with a termi-nal illness, think that we are in the clear for the time being. On the rare occasion that we think about death, we wonder, *How much will I inherit?* or *Where will they scatter my ashes?* In that sense we are unsophisticated.

After his third journey, Siddhartha became genuinely despondent over his powerlessness to protect his subjects, his parents, and most of all his beloved wife, Yashodhara, and son, Rahula, from unavoidable death. He had the means to prevent such miseries as poverty, hunger, and homelessness, but he could not shield them from old age and death. As he became consumed with these thoughts, Siddhartha attempted to discuss mortality with his father. The king was understandably puzzled that the prince was so caught up with what he regarded as a theoretical dilemma. Suddhodana was also increasingly worried that his son would ful-fill the prophecy and choose the path of asceticism instead of tak-ing his place as the rightful heir to the kingdom. In those days it was not unheard of for privileged and wealthy Hindus to become ascetics. Suddhodana outwardly tried to dismiss Siddhartha's fix-ation, but he had not forgotten the prophecy.

This was not a passing melancholic reflection. Siddhartha was obsessed. To prevent the prince from sinking deeper into his depression, Suddhodana told him not to leave the palace again, and secretly instructed the royal attendants to keep close watch on his son. In the meantime, like any concerned father, he did everything he could to make things right by concealing further evidence of death and decay from the prince's view.

BABY RATTLES AND OTHER DISTRACTIONS

In many ways we are all like Suddhodana. In our everyday lives we have this impulse to shield ourselves and others from the truth. We've become impervious to obvious signs of decay. We encourage ourselves by "not dwelling on it" and by employing positive affirmations. We celebrate our birthdays by blowing out candles, ignoring the fact that the extinguished candles could equally be seen as a reminder that we are a year closer to death. We celebrate the New Year with firecrackers and champagne, distracting ourselves from the fact that the old year will never come back and the new year is filled with uncertainty—anything can happen.

When that "anything" is displeasing, we deliberately divert our attention, like a mother distracting a child with rattles and toys. If we feel down, we go shopping, we treat ourselves, we go to the cinema. We build fantasies and aim for lifetime achievements—beach houses, plaques and trophies, early retirement, nice cars, good friends and family, fame, making it into *The Guinness Book of World Records*. Later in life we want a devoted companion with whom we can take a cruise or raise purebred poodles. Magazines and television introduce and reinforce such models of happiness and success, ever inventing new illusions to trap us. These notions of success are our grown-up baby rattles. Hardly anything we do in the course of a day—neither in our thoughts nor in our actions—indicates that we are aware of how fragile life is. We spend our time doing things like waiting at the multiplex for a bad movie to start. Or rushing home to watch reality TV. As we sit watching commercials, waiting . . . our time in this life ebbs away.

A rare glimpse of old age and death was enough to instill in Siddhartha a longing to be exposed to the truth in its entirety. After his third journey, he tried several times to leave the palace on his own, but always in vain. Then one remarkable night, after the usual evening of feasting and revelry, a mysterious spell swept through the court, overpowering all but Siddhartha. He wandered the halls and found that everyone, from King Suddhodana to the lowliest servants, had fallen into a deep sleep. Buddhists believe that this collective somnolence was due to the collective merit of all humans, because it was the inciting event that led to the creation of a great being.

Without the need to please the royals, the slack-jawed courtesans snored, their limbs akimbo, their jeweled fingers dropped in their curries. Like crushed flowers, they had lost their beauty. Siddhartha did not rush to make order as we might have done; this sight only strengthened his determination. The loss of their beauty was just more evidence of impermanence. As they slumbered, the prince was finally able to take his leave unobserved. With one last look at Yashodhara and Rahula, he crept out into the night.

In many ways we are like Siddhartha. We may not be princes with peacocks, but we do have careers and house cats and countless responsibilities. We have our own palaces—one-room apartments in the slums, split-levels in the suburbs, or penthouses in Paris—and our own Yashodharas and Rahulas. And things go awry all the time. Appliances break, the neighbors argue, the roof leaks. Our loved ones die; or maybe they just look like death in the morning before they wake up, their jaws as slack as those of Siddhartha's courtesans. Maybe they smell like stale cigarettes or last night's garlic sauce. They nag us, and they chew with their mouths open. Yet we are stuck there willingly, we don't try to escape. Or if we do get fed up and think, *Enough is enough,* we may leave a relationship, only to start all over again with another person. We never grow weary of this cycle because we have hope and belief that the perfect soul mate or a flawless Shangri-la is out there waiting for us. When faced with daily irritations, our reflex is to think that we can make it right: this is all fixable, teeth are brushable, we can feel whole.

Maybe we also think that some day we will have gained perfect maturity from the lessons of our lives. We expect to be wise old sages like Yoda, not realizing that maturity is just another aspect of decay. Subconsciously we are lured by the expectation that we will reach a stage where we don't have to fix anything ever again. One day we will reach "happily ever after." We are convinced of the notion of "resolution." It's as if everything that we've experienced up until now, our whole lives to this moment, was a dress rehearsal. We believe our grand performance is yet to come, so we do not live for today.

For most people this endless managing, rearranging, upgrading is the definition of "living." In reality, we are waiting for life to start. When prodded, most of us admit that we are working toward some future moment of perfection—retirement in a log cabin in Kennebunkport or in a hut in Costa Rica. Or maybe we dream of living out our later years in the idealized forest landscape of a Chinese painting, serenely meditating in a teahouse overlooking a waterfall and koi pond.

We also have a tendency to think that after we die, the world will go on. The same sun will shine and the same planets will rotate just as we think they have done since time began. Our children will inherit the earth. This shows how ignorant we are of the persistent shifting of this world and all phenomena. Children don't always outlive parents, and while they are alive they don't necessarily conform to our ideal. Your sweet little well-behaved kids can grow up into cocaine-snorting thugs who bring home all kinds of lovers. The straightest parents in the world produce some of the most flamboyant homosexuals, just as some of the most laid-back hippies end up with neoconservative children. Yet we still cling to the archetype of the family and the dream of having our bloodlines, jaw lines, surnames, and traditions carried on through our progeny.

SEEKING THE TRUTH CAN SEEM LIKE A BAD THING

It is important to recognize that the prince was not abandoning his domestic responsibilities; he wasn't evading the draft to join an organic farming community or to follow a romantic dream. He was leaving home with the determination of a husband sacrificing comfort in order to earn necessary and valuable provisions for his family, even if they did not see it so. We can only imagine Suddhodana's grief and disappointment the next morning. It was the same disappointment of modern parents who discover that their teenagers have run off to Kathmandu or Ibiza to chase some idealistic vision of utopia, like the flower children of the sixties (many of whom also came from comfortable, prosperous homes). Instead of donning bell-bottoms, piercings, purple hair dye, and tattoos, Siddhartha rebelled by removing his princely finery. Discarding these items that identified him as an educated aristocrat, he clothed himself in only a scrap of cloth and became a wandering mendicant.

Our society, so accustomed to judging people by what they have rather than who they are, would expect Siddhartha to stay in the palace, lead the privileged life, and carry on his family's name. The model of success in our world is Bill Gates. Rarely do we think in terms of the success of Gandhi. In certain Asian societies, as well as in the West, parents pressure their children to succeed in school far beyond what could be considered healthy. The children need good marks in order to be accepted to Ivy League schools, and they need Ivy League degrees to get high-ranking jobs at the bank. And all this is just so that the family can perpetuate its eternal dynasty.

Imagine that your son suddenly gives up his illustrious and lucrative career after becoming aware of death and old age. He no longer sees the point of working fourteen-hour days, sucking up to his boss, greedily swallowing up competitors, destroying the environment, contributing to child labor, and living in constant tension only to have a few weeks of vacation every year. He tells you that he wants to cash in his stocks, donate everything to an orphanage, and become a vagabond. What would you do? Give him your blessing and boast to your friends about how your son has come to his senses at last? Or would you tell him that he is being utterly irresponsible and send him to a psychiatrist?

Mere aversion to death and old age was not reason enough for the prince to turn his back on his palace life and step into the unknown. Siddhartha was drawn to take such drastic action because he could not rationalize the fact that this was the fate of all beings that had ever been born and ever would be born. If everything that is born must decay and die, then all the peacocks in the garden; the jewels, canopies, incense, and music; the golden tray that held his slippers; the imported carafes; his bond with Yashodhara and Rahula, his family, and his country were all meaningless. What was the purpose of all this? Why would any person of sound mind shed blood and tears for something that he knew would eventually evaporate or must be abandoned? How could he remain in the artificial bliss of his palace?

We may wonder where Siddhartha could go. Inside or outside the palace, there is no place to take refuge from death. All his royal wealth couldn't buy him an extension. Was he on a quest for immortality? We know that is futile. We are entertained by the fantastic myths of the immortal Greek gods, and the stories of the Holy Grail with its elixir of immortality, and Ponce de León leading the conquistadores on a fruitless search for the fountain of youth. We chuckle at the legendary Chinese emperor Qin Shi Huang who sent a delegation of virgin boys and girls to far-off lands to seek out potions that would confer long life. We might think that Siddhartha was after the same thing. It's true that he left the palace with some naïveté—he would not be able to make his wife and child live forever—but his search was not futile.

WHAT BUDDHA FOUND

Without a single scientific tool, Prince Siddhartha sat on a patch of *kusha* grass beneath a *ficus religiosa* tree investigating human nature. After a long time of contemplation, he came to the realization that all form, including our flesh and bones, and all our emotions and all our perceptions, are assembled—they are the product of two or more things coming together. When any two components or more come together, a new phenomenon emerges—nails and wood become a table; water and leaves become tea; [fear, devotion, and a savior become God.] This end product doesn't have an existence independent of its parts. Believing it truly exists independently is the greatest deception. Meanwhile the parts have undergone a change. Just by meeting, their character has changed and, together, they have become something else—they are "compounded."

He realized that this applies not only to the human experience but to all matter, the entire world, the universe—because everything is interdependent, everything is subject to change. Not one component in all creation exists in an autonomous, permanent, pure state. Not the book you are holding, not atoms, not even the gods. So as long as something exists within reach of our mind, even in our imagination, such as a man with four arms, then it depends on the existence of something else. Thus Siddhartha discovered that impermanence does not mean death, as we usually think, it means change. Anything that changes in relation to another thing: even the slightest shift, is subject to the laws of impermanence.

Through these realizations, Siddhartha found a way around the suffering of mortality after all. He accepted that change is inevitable and that death is just a part of this cycle. Furthermore, he realized that there was no almighty power who could reverse the path to death; therefore there was also no hope to trap him. If there is no blind hope, there is also no disappointment. If one knows that everything is impermanent, one does not grasp, and if one does not grasp, one will not think in terms of having or lacking, and therefore one lives fully.

Siddhartha's awakening from the illusion of permanence gives us reason to refer to him as the Buddha, the Awakened One. Now, 2,500 years later, we see that what he discovered and taught is a priceless treasure that has inspired millions—educated and illiterate, rich and poor, from King Ashoka to Allan Ginsberg, from Kublai Khan to Gandhi, from H. H. the Dalai Lama to the Beastie Boys. On the other hand, if Siddhartha were here today, he would be more than a little disappointed, because, for the most part, his discoveries lie fallow. That is not to say that modern technology is so great that his findings have been refuted: No one has become immortal. Everyone must die at some point; an estimated 250,000 human beings do so every day. People close to us have died and will die. Yet we are still shocked and saddened when a loved one passes away, and we continue to search for the fountain of youth or a secret formula for long life. Trips to the health food store, our bottles of DMAE and retinol, power yoga classes, Korean ginseng, plastic surgery, collagen injections, and moisturizing lotion—these are clear evidence that we secretly share Emperor Qin's desire for immortality.

Prince Siddhartha no longer needed or wanted the elixir of immortality. By realizing that all things are assembled, that deconstruction is infinite, and that not one of the components in all creation exists in an autonomous, permanent, pure state, he was liberated. Anything that is put together (which we now understand to be everything) and its impermanent nature are bound together as one, just like water and an ice cube. When we put an ice cube in our drink, we get both. Just so, when Siddhartha looked at someone walking around, even the healthiest person, he saw this person as both simultaneously living and disintegrating. You might think this doesn't sound like a fun way to live, but it can be an amazing ride to see both sides. There might be great satisfaction. It is not like a roller coaster of hope and disappointment going up and down. Seeing things in this way, they begin to dissolve all around us. Your perception of phenomena transforms, and in a way becomes clearer. It is so easy to see how people get caught up in the roller coaster, and you naturally have compassion for them. One of the reasons you have compassion is that impermanence is so obvious, yet they just don't see it.

"FOR NOW"-NESS

By nature, the act of assembly is bound by time—a beginning, a middle, and an end. This book did not exist before, it appears to exist now, and eventually it will fall apart. Similarly, the self that existed yesterday—that is, *you*—is different from the self that exists today. Your bad mood has become good, you may have learned something, you have new memories, the scrape on your knee has healed a little. Our seemingly continuous existence is a series of beginnings and endings bound by time. Even the very act of creation requires time: a time before existing, a time of coming into existence, and an end to the act of creation.

Those who believe in an almighty God generally do not analyze their concept of time, because God is assumed to be independent of time. To give credit to an all-powerful, omnipotent creator, we must factor in the element of time. If this world has always existed, there would be no need for creation. Therefore it must not have existed for a period of time before creation, and thus a sequence of time is required. Since the creator—let's say God—necessarily abides by the laws of time, he, too, must be subject to change, even if the only change he has ever gone through has been creating this one world. And that is fine. An omnipresent and permanent God cannot change, so it's better to have an impermanent God who can answer prayers and change the weather. But as long as God's actions are an assemblage of beginnings and ends, he is impermanent, in other words subject to uncertainty and unreliable.

If there is no paper, there is no book. If there is no water, there is no ice. If there is no beginning, there is no end. The existence of one very much depends on the other, therefore there is no such thing as true independence. Because of interdependence, if one component—the leg of a table, for example—makes even a small shift, then the integrity of the whole is compromised, unstable. Although we think that we can control change, most of the time it's not possible because of the countless unseen influences of which we are unaware. And because of this interdependence, the disintegration of all things in their current or original state is inevitable. Every change contains within it an element of death. Today is the death of yesterday.

Most people accept that everything born must eventually die; however, our definitions of "everything" and "death" may differ. For Siddhartha, *birth* refers to all creation—not just flowers and mushrooms and human beings, but everything that is born or assembled in any way. And *death* refers to any kind of disintegration or disassembly. Siddhartha had no research grants or assistants, just the hot Indian dust and a few passing water buffalo as witnesses. So equipped, he realized the truth of impermanence on a profound level. His realization was not as spectacular as finding a new star, it was not designed to propound moral judgments or to establish a social movement or religion, nor was it a prophecy. Impermanence is a simple mundane fact; it's highly unlikely that one of these days, some mischievous compounded thing will become permanent. Even less likely would be our ability to prove such a thing. Yet today we either deify Buddha or try to outsmart Buddha with our advanced technology.

AND YET WE STILL IGNORE IT

Two thousand five-hundred thirty-eight years after Siddhartha walked out the palace door—at the time of year when many millions of people are celebrating, making merry, and anticipating a fresh start, the time to remember God for some, the time to take advantage of discount sales for others—a catastrophic tsunami shook the world. Even the most coldhearted of us gasped in horror. As the story unfolded on television, some of us wished that Orson Welles would interrupt to announce that it was all a fabrication, or that Spiderman would sweep down to save the day.

There is no doubt that Prince Siddhartha's heart would have broken to see the tsunami victims washed ashore. But his heart would have been even more broken by the fact that we were taken by surprise, proof of our constant denial of impermanence. This planet is made of volatile magma. Every land mass—Australia, Taiwan, the Americas—is like dew, about to drop from the grass. Yet construction of skyscrapers and tunnels never stops. Our insatiable deforestation for the sake of disposable chopsticks and junk mail only invites impermanence to act more quickly. It should not surprise us to see signs of the end of any given phenomenon, but we are very difficult to convince.

Yet even after a devastating reminder like the tsunami, the death and devastation will soon be camouflaged and forgotten. Luxurious resorts will be erected on the very spot where families came to identify the corpses of their loved ones. The people of the world will continue to be caught up in compounding and fabricating reality with hopes of achieving long-lasting happiness. Wishing for "happily ever after" is nothing more than a desire for permanence in disguise. Fabricating concepts such as "eternal love," "everlasting happiness," and "salvation" generates more evidence of impermanence. Our intention and the result are at odds. We intend to establish ourselves and our world, but we forget that the corrosion begins as soon as creation begins. What we aim for is not decay, but what we do leads directly to decay.

At the very least, Buddha advised, we must try to keep the concept of impermanence in mind and not knowingly conceal it. By maintaining our awareness of assembled phenomena, we become aware of interdependence. Recognizing interdependence, we recognize impermanence. And when we remember that things are impermanent, we are less likely to be enslaved by assumptions, rigid beliefs (both religious and secular), value systems, or blind faith. Such awareness prevents us from getting caught up in all kinds of personal, political, and relationship dramas. We begin to know that things are not entirely under our control and never will be, so there is no expectation for things to go according to our hopes and fears. There is no one to blame when things go wrong because there are countless causes and conditions to blame. We can direct this awareness from the farthest regions of our imaginations to subatomic levels. Even atoms cannot be trusted.

INSTABILITY

This planet Earth you are sitting on right now as you read this book will eventually become as lifeless as Mars—if it's not shattered by a meteor first. Or a supervolcano might obscure the sun's light, extinguishing all life on Earth. Many of the stars that we romantically gaze at in the night sky are already long gone; we are enjoying the rays from stars that expired a million light-years ago. On the surface of this fragile Earth, the continents are still shifting. Three hundred million years ago the American continents that we now know were part of a single supercontinent that geologists call Pangaea.

But we don't have to wait 300 million years to see change. Even within one short life span we have witnessed the grandiose concept of empires fade away like a water spot on hot sand. For example, India used to have an empress who lived in England and whose flag waved in countries around the globe. But today the sun *does* set on the Union Jack. The so-called nationalities and races with which we so strongly identify are ever-changing. For example, warriors such as the Maori and Navajo, who once ruled their territories for hundreds of years, now live as minorities on cramped reservations, while immigrants who have settled from Europe in the last 250 years are the ruling majorities. Han Chinese used to refer to the Manchu people as "them," but China has since decided it is a republic comprising many ethnic groups, so now the Manchu are "us." However, this constant transformation hasn't stopped us from sacrificing life and limb to establish powerful nations, borders, and societies. How much blood has been shed in the name of political systems over the centuries? Each system is shaped by and assembled from innumerable unstable factors—the economy, harvests, personal ambition, the cardiovascular condition of a leader, lust, love, and luck. Legendary leaders are also unstable: some fall from grace because they smoke but don't inhale; others come into power because of hanging chads.

The complexity of impermanence and the instability of all compounded phenomena only increases within the realm of international relations, because the definitions of "ally" and "enemy" are constantly shifting. There was a time when America blindly lashed out at an enemy called "communism." Even Che Guevara, a great social hero, was condemned as a terrorist because he belonged to a certain party and wore a red star on his beret. He very well may not even have been the perfect communist we painted him to be. A few decades later, the White House now woos China, the single largest communist country, granting her "Most Favored Nation" status and turning a blind eye to the very things that used to merit an American battle cry.

It must be because of the volatile nature of foes and friends that when Channa begged to attend Siddhartha on his quest for the truth, Siddhartha refused. Even his closest confident and friend was subject to change. We often experience changing alliances in personal relationships. The best friend with whom you have shared your deepest secrets has the power to become your worst enemy because he or she can turn that intimacy against you. President Bush, Osama Bin Laden, and Saddam Hussein had a big messy public breakup. The trio had long enjoyed a cozy relationship, but now they have become the very model of archenemies. Using their intimate knowledge of one another, they have commenced a bloody crusade, costing many thousands of lives, in order to enforce their different versions of "morality."

Because we are proud of our principles and often impose them on others, this concept of morality still holds a wisp of value. However, the definition of "morality" has changed throughout human history, shifting according to the zeitgeist of the era. America's ever-fluctuating barometer of what is politically correct or incorrect is mind-boggling. No matter how one refers to the various races and cultural groups, someone is bound to get offended. The rules keep changing. One day we invite a friend to dinner, and since he is a fanatical vegetarian, we have to tailor the menu to him. But then the next time he comes over, he asks where's the meat because now he is a fanatical protein-diet practitioner. Or someone who advocates abstinence before marriage can suddenly become very promiscuous once he or she tries it once.

Ancient Asian art depicts women walking bare-breasted, and even in recent history some Asian societies found it acceptable for women to go without a top. Then the assembled phenomena of television and Western values ushered in a new ethic. Suddenly it's morally wrong to go braless; if you don't cover your breasts, you're considered vulgar and can even be arrested. Once–free-spirited countries now busy themselves adopting this and other new ethics, ordering bras and covering up as much as possible even during the hottest monsoon. The breast isn't inherently bad, the breast hasn't changed, but the morals have. The change transforms the breast into something sinful, leading the U.S. Federal Communications Commission to fine CBS $550,000 for Janet Jackson's three-second exposure of just one of her mammaries.

CAUSES AND CONDITIONS: THE EGG IS COOKED AND THERE IS NOTHING YOU CAN DO ABOUT IT

When Siddhartha spoke of "all assembled things," he was referring to more than just obvious perceptible phenomena such as DNA, your dog, the Eiffel Tower, eggs, and sperm. Mind, time, memory, and God are also assembled. And each assembled component in turn depends on several layers of assembly. Similarly, when he taught impermanence, he went beyond conventional thinking about "the end," such as the notion that death happens once and then it's over. Death is continuous from the moment of birth, from the moment of creation. Each change is a form of death, and therefore each birth contains the death of something else. Consider cooking a hen's egg. Without constant change, the cooking of an egg cannot occur. The cooked-egg result requires some fundamental causes and conditions. Obviously you need an egg, a pot of water, and some sort of heating element. And then there are some not-so-essential causes and conditions, such as a kitchen, lights, an egg timer, a hand to put the egg into the pot. Another important condition is absence of interruption, such as a power outage or a goat walking in and overturning the pot. Furthermore, each condition—the hen, for example—requires another set of causes and conditions. It needs another hen to lay an egg so that it can be born, a safe place for this to happen, and food to help it grow. The chicken feed has to be grown somewhere and must make its way into the chicken. We can keep breaking down the indispensable and dispensable requirements all the way to the subatomic level, with an ever-increasing number of forms, shapes, functions, and labels.

When all the innumerable causes and conditions come together, and there is no obstacle or interruption, the result is inevitable. Many misunderstand this to be fate or luck, but we still do have the power to have an effect on conditions, at least in the beginning. But at a certain point, even if we pray that the egg won't cook, it will be cooked.

Like the egg, *all* phenomena are the product of myriad components, and therefore they are variable. Nearly all of these myriad components are beyond our control, and for that reason they defy our expectations. The least-promising presidential candidate might win the election and then lead the country to contentment and prosperity. The candidate you campaign for might win and then lead the country to economic and social ruin, making your life miserable. You may think liberal, left-wing politics are enlightened politics, but they may actually be the cause of fascism and skinheads by being complacent or even promoting tolerance of the intolerant. Or by protecting the individual rights of those whose sole purpose is to destroy other people's individual rights. The same unpredictability applies to all forms, feelings, perceptions, traditions, love, trust, mistrust, skepticism—even the relationships between spiritual masters and disciples, and between men and their gods.

All of these phenomena are impermanent. Take skepticism, for example. There was once a Canadian man who was the very embodiment of a skeptic. He enjoyed attending Buddhist teachings so that he could argue with the teachers. He was actually quite well versed in Buddhist philosophy, so his arguments were strong. He relished the opportunity to quote the Buddhist teaching that the Buddha's words must be analyzed and not taken for granted. A few years later, and he is now the devoted follower of a famous psychic channeler. The ultimate skeptic sits before his singing guru with tears running like rivers from his eyes, devoted to an entity who has not a scrap of logic to offer. Faith or devotion has a general connotation of being unwavering, but like skepticism and like all compounded phenomena, is impermanent.

Whether you pride yourself on your religion or on not belonging to any religion, faith plays an important role in your existence. Even "not believing" requires faith—total, blind faith in your own logic or reason based on your ever-changing feelings. So it is no surprise when what used to seem so convincing no longer persuades us. The illogical nature of faith is not subtle at all; in fact it is among the most assembled and interdependent of phenomena. Faith can be triggered by the right look at the right time in the right place. Your faith may depend on superficial compatibility. Let's say that you are a misogynist and you meet a person who is preaching hatred against women. You will find that person powerful, you will agree with him, and you will have some faith in him. Something as inconsequential as a shared love of anchovies might add to your devotion. Or perhaps a person or institution has the ability to lessen your fear of the unknown. Other factors such as the family, country, or society you are born into are all part of the assembly of elements that come together as what we call faith.

Citizens of many Buddhist-ruled countries, such as Bhutan, Korea, Japan, and Thailand, are blindly committed to the Buddhist doctrine. On the other hand, many young people in those countries become disillusioned with Buddhism because there is not enough information and too many distractions for the phenomena of faith to stick, and they end up following another faith, or following their own reason.

IMPERMANENCE WORKS FOR US

There are many benefits to understanding the notion of assembly, how creating even one boiled egg involves such a vast number of phenomena. When we learn to see the assembled parts of all things and situations, we learn to cultivate forgiveness, understanding, open-mindedness, and fearlessness. For example, some people still single out Mark Chapman as the sole culprit in John Lennon's murder. Perhaps if our celebrity worship were not so great, Mark Chapman would not have created the fantasy of killing John Lennon. Twenty years after the fact, Chapman admitted that when he shot John Lennon, he didn't see him as a real human being. His mental instability was due to a large number of assembled factors (brain chemistry, upbringing, the U.S. mental health care system). When we can see how a sick and tormented mind is assembled, and recognize the conditions under which it is operating, then we are better able to understand and forgive the Mark Chapmans of the world. As in the case of the boiled egg, even if we were to pray for the assassination not to be, it would have been inevitable.

But perhaps even with this understanding, we still fear Mark Chapman because of his unpredictability. Fear and anxiety are the dominant psychological states of the human mind. Behind the fear lies a constant longing to be certain. We are afraid of the unknown. The mind's craving for confirmation is rooted in our fear of impermanence.

Fearlessness is generated when you can appreciate uncertainty, when you have faith in the impossibility of these interconnected components remaining static and permanent. You will find yourself, in a very true sense, preparing for the worst while allowing for the best. You become dignified and majestic. These qualities enhance your ability to work, wage war, make peace, create a family, and enjoy love and personal relationships. By knowing that something is lying in wait for you just around the bend, by accepting that countless potentialities exist from this moment forward, you acquire the skill of pervasive awareness and foresight like that of a gifted general, not paranoid but prepared.

For Siddhartha, if there is no impermanence, there is no progress or change for the better. Dumbo, the flying elephant, came to understand this. As a youngster he was an outcast because of his enormous ears. He was lonely, depressed, and afraid that he would be kicked out of the circus. But then he discovered that his "deformity" was unique and valuable because it enabled him to fly. He became popular. Had he trusted impermanence to begin with, he would not have suffered so much in the beginning. The recognition of impermanence is the key to freedom from fear of remaining forever stuck in a situation, habit, or pattern.

Personal relationships are the most volatile and perfect examples of assembled phenomena and impermanence. Some couples believe that they can manage their relationship "until death do us part" by reading books or consulting with a relationship doctor. Knowing that men are from Mars and women are from Venus provides the key to only a few obvious causes and conditions of disharmony, however. To a certain extent these small understandings may help create temporary peace, but they don't address the many hidden factors that are part of the relationship's assembly. If we could see the unseen, then maybe we could enjoy the perfect relationship—or maybe we would never start one in the first place.

Applying Siddhartha's understanding of impermanence to relationships leads us to a pleasure described in Juliet's poignant words to Romeo: "Parting is such sweet sorrow . . ." Parting moments are often the most profound in a relationship. Every relationship must end eventually, even if it is because of death. Thinking this, our appreciation for the causes and conditions that have provided each connection is heightened. It is especially powerful if one partner has a terminal illness. There is no illusion of "forever," and that is surprisingly liberating; our caring and affection become unconditional and our joy is very much in the present. Giving love and support is more effortless and satisfying when our partner's days are numbered.

But we forget that our days are *always* numbered. Even if we understand intellectually that everything born must die and that everything assembled will eventually disintegrate, in our emotional state we constantly slip back into operating out of a belief in permanence, entirely forgetting interdependence. This habit can foster all kinds of negative states: paranoia, loneliness, guilt. We may feel put upon, threatened, mistreated, neglected—as if this world were unjust to us alone.

BEAUTY IS IN THE EYE OF THE BEHOLDER

When Siddhartha left Kapilavastu, he was not alone. In the predawn hours, as his family and servants slept, he went to the stable, where Channa, his chariot driver and most trusted friend, slept. Channa was speechless at the sight of Siddhartha unattended, but at his master's instruction, he saddled Siddhartha's favorite steed, Kathanka. They passed through the city gates undetected. When they were a safe distance away, Siddhartha dismounted and proceeded to remove all of his bangles, anklets, and princely finery. These he gave to Channa, ordering him to take Kathanka and return to the city. Channa pleaded to be allowed to accompany Siddhartha, but the prince was firm. Channa was to go back and continue to serve the royal family.

Siddhartha asked Channa to convey a message to his family. They were not to worry about him, because he was embarking on a very important journey. He had already given Channa all his ornaments but one, the final symbol of splendor, caste, and royal bearing—his beautiful long hair. This he cut himself and, handing it to Channa, he set off alone. Siddhartha was embarking on his exploration of impermanence. Already it seemed foolish to him to put so much energy into beauty and vanity. He was not critical of beauty and good grooming, only of the belief in their essential permanence.

It is often said that "beauty is in the eye of the beholder." This statement is more profound than it may at first appear. The concept of beauty is fickle; the causes and conditions of fashion trends continually change, just as the beholders of the trend continually change. As late as the mid-twentieth century, the feet of young girls in China were bound so that they would grow no more than three or four inches long. The results of this torture were considered beautiful; men even found erotic pleasure in the stench of the cloths that were used to bind the feet. Now Chinese ladies are going through other forms of suffering, having their shins extended so that they can look like women from *Vogue*. Indian girls starve themselves to reduce their voluptuous figures—so full and comely in Ajanta's paintings—to the angular lines of Parisian models. Silent film stars in the West were celebrated for having lips smaller than their eyes, but today the fashion is for large mouths with sausage lips. Perhaps the next charismatic celebrity will have lizard lips and parrot eyes. Then all those women with puffed-up lips will have to pay for lip reductions.

IMPERMANENCE IS GOOD NEWS

Buddha was not a pessimist or a doomsayer; he was a realist, while we tend to be escapists. When he stated that all assembled things are impermanent, he did not intend for that to be bad news; it is a simple, scientific fact. Depending on your perspective and on your understanding of this fact, it can become a gateway to inspiration and hope, glory and success. For example, to the extent that global warming and poverty are products of insatiable capitalistic conditions, these misfortunes can be reversed. This is thanks to the impermanent nature of assembled phenomena. Instead of depending on supernatural powers, such as God's will, to reverse such negative trends, a simple understanding of the nature of assembled phenomena is all that is needed. When you understand phenomena, you can manipulate them, and thus affect causes and conditions. You might be surprised how much a small step like just saying no to plastic bags would postpone global warming.

Recognizing the instability of causes and conditions leads us to understand our own power to transform obstacles and make the impossible possible. This is true in every area of life. If you don't have a Ferrari, you very well may create the conditions to have one. As long as there is a Ferrari, there is the opportunity for you to own one. Likewise if you want to live longer, you can choose to stop smoking and exercise more. There is reasonable hope. Hopelessness—just like its opposite, blind hope—is the result of a belief in permanence.

You can transform not only your physical world but your emotional world, for example, turning agitation into peace of mind by letting go of ambition or turning low self-respect into confidence by acting out of kindness and philanthropy. If we all condition ourselves to put our feet in other people's shoes, we will cultivate peace in our homes, with our neighbors, and with other countries.

These are all examples of how we can affect assembled phenomena on a mundane level. Siddhartha also found that even the most feared levels of hell and damnation are impermanent because they, too, are assembled. Hell does not exist as a permanent state somewhere underground, where the damned suffer eternal torture. It is more like a nightmare. A dream in which an elephant tramples you comes about because of a number of conditions—first of all sleep, and perhaps you have some negative history with elephants. It doesn't matter how long the nightmare lasts; during that time you are in hell. Then, because of the causes and conditions of an alarm clock or because you simply have finished sleeping, you wake up. The dream is a temporary hell, and it is not unlike our concepts of a "real" hell.

Similarly, if you have hatred toward a person and engage in acts of aggression or revenge, that in itself is an experience of hell. Hatred, political manipulation, and revenge have caused hell on this earth, for example when a young boy—shorter, thinner, and lighter than the AK-47 he carries—does not have even one day's opportunity to play or celebrate his birthday because he is too busy being a soldier. This is none other than hell. We have these kinds of hells because of causes and conditions, and therefore we can also exit these hells by using love and compassion as antidotes to anger and hatred, as Buddha prescribed.

The concept of impermanence does not foretell Armageddon or the Apocalypse, nor is it a punishment for our sins. It is not inherently negative or positive, it is simply part of the process of the compounding of things. We usually appreciate only half of the cycle of impermanence. We can accept birth but not death, accept gain but not loss, or the end of exams but not the beginning. True liberation comes from appreciating the whole cycle and not grasping onto those things that we find agreeable. By remembering the changeability and impermanence of causes and conditions, both positive and negative, we can use them to our advantage. Wealth, health, peace, and fame are just as temporary as their opposites. And of course Siddhartha wasn't favoring heaven and heavenly experiences. They are equally impermanent.

We might wonder why Siddhartha said that "all *assembled* things" are impermanent. Why not just say that "all things" are impermanent? It would be correct to say that all things are impermanent without the qualifying word *assembled*. However, we must take every opportunity to remind ourselves of the first part, the assembly, in order to maintain the logic behind the statement. "Assembly" is a very simple concept, yet it has so many layers that to understand it deeply, we need this constant reminder.

Nothing that exists or functions in the world, no constructs of the imagination or of the physical plane, nothing that passes through your mind, not even your mind itself, will stay as it is forever. Things might last for the duration of your experience of this existence, or even into the next generation; but then again, they may dissolve sooner than you expect. Either way, eventual change is inevitable. There is no degree of probability or chance involved. If you feel hopeless, remember this and you will no longer have a reason to be hopeless, because whatever is causing you to despair will also change. Everything must change. It is not inconceivable that Australia will become part of China, Holland will become part of Turkey. It is not inconceivable that you will cause the death of another human being or be bound to a wheelchair. You may become a millionaire, or a savior of all humankind, or a Nobel Peace Prize laureate, or an enlightened being.

two

Emotion and Pain

Through many years of contemplation and penance, Siddhartha remained steadfast in his determination to find the root cause of suffering and to ease his own suffering and the suffering of others. He headed to Magadha, in the heart of India, to continue his meditation. Along the way he met a grass seller named Sotthiya, who offered him a handful of kusha grass. Siddhartha recognized this as an auspicious sign; in ancient Indian culture, kusha grass was considered a cleansing substance. Instead of continuing his journey, he decided to stop and meditate right there. He found a place to sit on the flat stones under a nearby *ficus religiosa* tree, using the kusha grass as a mat. Silently he vowed, *This body may rot, I may disintegrate into the dust, but until I find the answer, I will not rise.*

As Siddhartha sat in contemplation beneath the tree, he did not go unnoticed. Mara, the king of the demons, heard Siddhartha's vow and sensed the strength of his resolve. Mara grew sleepless, for he knew that within Siddhartha existed the potential to throw his entire domain into chaos. Being a strategic warrior, he sent five of his most beautiful daughters to distract and seduce the prince. As the girls (we call them *apsara*s, or nymphs) set out, they had full confidence in their seductive talents. But as they approached the meditating Siddhartha, their beauty began to vanish. They withered and aged, they grew warts, and a stench rose from their skin. Siddhartha did not stir. The dejected apsaras returned to their father, who was furious. How dare anyone refuse his daughters! In his rage, Mara summoned his retinue, a great army furnished with every imaginable weapon.

Mara's army attacked in full force. But to their dismay, all the arrows, spears, stones, and catapults aimed at Siddhartha transformed into a rain of flowers as soon as they came within reach of their target. After many long hours of unsuccessful warfare, Mara and his army were exhausted and defeated. Finally Mara came to Siddhartha and, with all his diplomacy, tried to talk him into giving up his quest. Siddhartha said he could not give up after all these lifetimes of trying. Mara asked, *How can we be so sure you have been struggling for so long?* Siddhartha answered, *I don't need validation, the earth is my witness*, and with this he touched the ground, the earth shook, and Mara evaporated into thin air. Thus Siddhartha found liberation and became a buddha. He had discovered the path to end suffering at its very root, not only for himself but for all people. The place of his final battle against Mara is now called Bodh Gaya, and the tree under which he sat is called "the bodhi tree."

This is the story that Buddhist mothers have told their children for many generations.

DEFINING PERSONAL HAPPINESS

It is not appropriate to ask a Buddhist, "What is the purpose of life?" because the question suggests that somewhere out there, perhaps in a cave or on a mountaintop, an ultimate purpose exists. The question suggests that we could decode the secret by studying with living saints, reading books, or mastering esoteric practices. If the question is based on an assumption that aeons ago someone, or some god, designed a diagram of the purpose, then it is a theistic question. Buddhists don't believe that there is an almighty creator, and they don't have this concept that the purpose of life has been, or needs to be, decided and defined.

A more appropriate question to ask a Buddhist is simply, "What is life?" From our understanding of impermanence, the answer should be obvious: "Life is a big array of assembled phenomena, and thus life is impermanent." It is a constant shifting, a collection of transitory experiences. And although myriad life-forms exist, one thing we all have in common is that no living being wishes to suffer. We all want to be happy, from presidents and billionaires to hardworking ants, bees, prawns, and butterflies.

Of course, the definitions of "suffering" and "happiness" differ a great deal among these life-forms, even within the relatively small human realm. The definition of "suffering" for some is the definition of "happiness" for others and vice versa. For some humans, being happy means just managing to survive; for others it means owning seven hundred pairs of shoes. There are those who find happiness in having a likeness of David Beckham tattooed on their biceps. Sometimes the price is the life of another being, as when one's happiness depends on getting hold of a shark's fin, a chicken's thigh, or a tiger's penis. Some consider the gentle tickle of a feather erotic, while others prefer cheese graters, whips, and chains. King Edward VIII preferred to marry an American divorcée instead of wearing the crown of the mighty British Empire.

Even within one individual, the definitions of "happiness" and "suffering" fluctuate. A light-hearted moment of flirtation can suddenly switch when one person desires a more serious relationship; hope turns into fear. When you are a child at the beach, making sand castles is happiness. As a teenager, watching the girls in their bikinis and the bare-chested surfer boys is happiness. In midlife, money and a career are happiness. And when you are in your late eighties, collecting ceramic salt shakers is happiness. For many, catering to these infinite and ever-changing definitions is the "purpose of life."

Many of us learn the definitions of "happiness" and "suffering" from the society in which we live; the social order dictates how we measure contentment. It is a matter of shared values. Two human beings from opposite sides of the world can experience identical feelings—pleasure, disgust, fear—based on contradictory cultural indicators of happiness. Chicken feet are a delicacy for the Chinese, while the French love to spread the exploding livers of geese on their toast. Imagine how the world would be if capitalism had never existed and every nation and individual truly lived Mao Tse-tung's pragmatic communist philosophy: we would be perfectly happy with no shopping malls, no posh cars, no Starbucks, no competition, no large gap between the poor and the rich, health care for all—and bicycles would be more valuable than Humvees. Instead, we learn what to want. A decade ago, videocassette recorders were the definitive symbol of affluence in the remote Himalayan kingdom of Bhutan. Gradually the Toyota Land Cruiser club has replaced the VCR club as Bhutan's ultimate vision of prosperity and happiness.

This habit of considering that the group's standards are our standards is formed at a very early age. In first grade you see that all the other children have a certain kind of pencil case. You develop a "need" to own one, to be like everyone else. You tell your mother, and whether or not she buys you that pencil case dictates your level of happiness. This continues into your adult life. The next-door neighbors have a plasma TV or a new SUV, so you want the same thing—only bigger and newer. Competition and desire for what others have also exist on a cultural level. Often we value another culture's customs and traditions more highly than our own. Recently a teacher in Taiwan decided to wear his hair long, as was the custom in China for centuries. He looked elegant, like an ancient Chinese warrior, but the school principal threatened to fire him if he didn't conform to "proper behavior," meaning a twenty-first-century Western-style short haircut. Now his cropped hair looks as if he had received an electric shock.

It's quite amazing to witness the Chinese being embarrassed by their own roots, yet we see many such cases of Asia's superiority-inferiority complex. On the one hand, Asians are so proud of their culture, yet on the other, they find it somehow offensive or backward. They have replaced it with Western culture in nearly all spheres of life—dress, music, morals, and even Western-style political systems.

On both personal and cultural levels, we adopt foreign or external methods to achieve happiness and overcome suffering, seldom realizing that these methods often bring about the opposite of the intended result. Our failure to adapt creates a new set of miseries because not only are we still suffering, we also feel alienated from our own lives, unable to fit into the system.

Some of these cultural definitions of "happiness" do work to an extent. In a general sense, having a bit of money in the bank, comfortable shelter, enough food to eat, decent shoes, and other basic comforts does make us happy. But then again, the sadhus of India and wandering hermits of Tibet feel happy because they have no need for a key ring—they have no fear that their possessions will be stolen because they have nothing to be locked up.

INSTITUTIONALIZED DEFINITIONS OF "HAPPINESS"

Long before he reached the famous spot in Bodh Gaya, Siddhartha sat under a different tree for six years. He grew emaciated on a diet of a few grains of rice and a few drops of water; he didn't bathe or cut his nails; and thus he became a model for his colleagues, the other spiritual seekers with whom he was practicing. He was so disciplined that the local cowherd children, who tickled his ears with grass and blew trumpets in his face, never succeeded in stirring him. But then one day, after many years of extreme deprivation, he realized, *This is not right. This is an extreme path, just another trap like the courtesans, peacock gardens, and jeweled spoons.* And he decided to rise from that state of penance and bathe in the nearby Nairanjana River (now known as the Phalgu). To the utter shock of his companions, he even accepted some fresh milk from a milkmaid named Sujata. It is believed that they deserted Siddhartha, thinking he was a bad moral influence and that being with him would impede their practice.

One can understand why these ascetics deserted Siddhartha for breaking his vows. Humans have always tried to find happiness not only through material gain but through spiritual means as well. Much of world history revolves around religion. Religions unite people with their illuminating paths and codes of conduct—loving your neighbor, practicing generosity and the Golden Rule, meditation, fasting, and making sacrifices. But these seemingly helpful principles can become extreme, puritanical dogma, causing people to feel unnecessary guilt and low self-esteem. It is not uncommon for the devout to arrogantly look down on other religions with complete intolerance, using their beliefs to justify cultural or even physical genocide. Examples of this kind of destructive devotion are numerous and pervasive.

Human beings rely not only on organized religion but on conventional wisdom—or even political slogans—to achieve happiness and alleviate their suffering. Theodore Roosevelt said, "If I must choose between righteousness and peace, I choose righteousness." But whose righteousness? Whose interpretation are we supposed to follow? Extremism is simply a matter of choosing one form of righteousness to the exclusion of all others.

As another example, it's easy to see the attraction of the wisdom of Confucius, such as respecting and obeying elders and not revealing the flaws and indignities of family and nation. His wisdom is very pragmatic and can be useful in functioning in this world. These may be wise guidelines, but in many cases these rules have resulted in extremely negative consequences, such as censorship and the suppression of opposing views. For example, the obsession with "saving face" and obeying elders has resulted in centuries of deception and lying, to next-door neighbors and to entire nations.

Given that history, the deep-seated hypocrisy of many Asian countries, such as China and Singapore, isn't surprising. The leaders of many countries condemn feudalism and monarchies and boast of adopting democracy or communism. But those same leaders, whose subjects revere them and whose misdeeds are kept secret, will hold office until their last breath, or until a hand-picked heir takes over. Little has changed from the old feudal systems. Law and justice are designed to keep the peace and create harmonious society, but in many cases the criminal justice system works to the advantage of the crooks and the wealthy, while the poor and the innocent suffer from unfair laws.

We human beings occupy ourselves with the pursuit of happiness and the cessation of suffering more than we do any other hobby or profession, employing innumerable methods and materials. This is why we have elevators, laptop computers, rechargeable batteries, electric dishwashers, toasters that shoot bread out so there is just the right amount of crust for you to grasp, dog shit vacuums, battery-operated nose hair clippers, toilets with heated seats, Novocain, mobile phones, Viagra, wall-to-wall carpeting. . . . But inevitably these conveniences provide an equal measure of headache.

Nations pursue happiness and the cessation of suffering on a grand scale, fighting for territory, oil, space, financial markets, and power. They wage preemptive wars to prevent anticipated suffering. Individually, we do the same thing by getting preventive medical care, taking vitamins, going to the doctor for vaccines and blood tests, and getting CAT scans of our entire bodies. We are searching for signs of impending suffering. And once we find the suffering, we immediately try to find the cure. Each year new techniques, remedies, and self-help books attempt to provide long-lasting solutions for suffering and, ideally, to eliminate the problem at its root.

Siddhartha was also trying to cut suffering at its root. But he was not dreaming up solutions such as starting a political revolution, migrating to another planet, or creating a new world economy. He wasn't even thinking about creating a religion or developing codes of conduct that would bring peace and harmony. He explored suffering with an open mind, and through his tireless contemplation Siddhartha discovered that at the root, it is our emotions that lead to suffering. In fact they *are* suffering. One way or another, directly or indirectly, all emotions are born from self-ishness in the sense that they involve clinging to the self. Moreover, he discovered that, as real as they may seem, emotions are not an inherent part of one's being. They are not inborn, nor are they some sort of curse or implant that someone or some god has thrust upon us. Emotions arise when particular causes and conditions come together, such as when you rush to think that someone is criticizing you, ignoring you, or depriving you of some gain. Then the corresponding emotions arise. The moment we accept those emotions, the moment we buy into them, we have lost awareness and sanity. We are "worked up." Thus Siddhartha found his solution—awareness. If you seriously wish to eliminate suffering, you must generate awareness, tend to your emotions, and learn how to avoid getting worked up.

If you examine emotions as Siddhartha did, if you try to identify their origin, you will find that they are rooted in misunderstanding and thus fundamentally flawed. All emotions are basically a form of prejudice; within each emotion there is always an element of judgment.

For example, a torch that is spun around at a certain speed appears as a circle of fire. At the circus, innocent children, and even some adults, find the spectacle entertaining and enchanting. Very young children don't separate the hand from the fire from the torch. They think that what they see is real; the optical illusion of the ring carries them away. However long it lasts, even if for just a moment, they are completely and deeply convinced. In a similar manner, many of us are deluded about the appearance of our own bodies. When we look at the body, we don't think in terms of its separate pieces: molecules, genes, veins, and blood. We think of the body as a whole; and moreover, we prejudge that this is a truly existing organism called "the body." Being convinced of this, we first wish for a flat tummy, artistic hands, imposing height, dark and handsome features, or a curvy figure. Then we become obsessed, investing in gym memberships, moisturizers, slimming tea, the South Beach Diet, yoga, crunches, and lavender-scented oil.

Just like children who are absorbed, thrilled, or even frightened by the ring of fire, we experience emotions toward our bodies' appearance and well-being. When it comes to a fire ring, adults generally know that it is merely an illusion, so we don't get worked up. Using basic reason, we can see that the ring is created from its assembled parts—the movement of a hand holding a flaming torch. A restless older sibling might become arrogant or patronizing toward the young child. Yet because, as mature adults, we can see the ring, we can understand the child's fascination, especially if it's nighttime and dancers, trance music, and other commotion accompany the spectacle. Then it might even provide a thrill for us adults, despite our awareness of its essentially illusory quality. According to Siddhartha, this understanding is the seed of compassion.

THE UNCOUNTABLE ASSORTMENT OF EMOTIONS

As his meditation deepened, Siddhartha began to see the essentially illusory quality of all phenomena, and with this understanding he looked back upon his former life at the palace, the parties and peacock gardens, his friends and family. He saw that the so-called family is like a guesthouse or hotel where different travelers have checked in and temporarily bonded. Eventually this conglomeration of beings disperses—at the time of death, if not sooner. While together, the group may develop a connection that involves trust, responsibility, love, and shared measures of success and failure, from which all sorts of dramas arise.

Siddhartha could see clearly how easy it is for people to become swept away by the notion of an idyllic family life, the idea of togetherness, and all the fascinating phenomena of palace life. Others did not see as he did, or as an adult seeing the fire ring might, that it is all just illusory, assembled, essenceless parts. But like a kind parent, instead of becoming arrogant or patronizing at their fascination, he saw that within this cycle there is no bad and no good; there is no fault, so there is no blame; and that freed him to feel only great compassion.

Seeing beyond the superficiality of palace life, Siddhartha could now see his own physical body as essenceless. To him the fire ring and the body have the same nature. As long as one believes that such things truly exist—either momentarily or "for all eternity"—one's belief is rooted in misunderstanding. This misunderstanding is none other than a lack of awareness. And when awareness is lost, that is what Buddhists call ignorance. It is from this ignorance that our emotions emerge. This process, from the loss of awareness to the emergence of emotions, can be fully explained using the four truths, as we will see.

An unfathomable variety of emotions exists in this worldly realm. Every moment, countless emotions are produced based on our misjudgments, prejudices, and ignorance. We are familiar with love and hate, guilt and innocence, devotion, pessimism, jealousy and pride, fear, shame, sadness, and joy, but there are so many more. Some cultures have words for emotions that in other cultures are undefined and therefore do not exist. In some parts of Asia, there is no word for romantic love, whereas the Spaniards have numerous words for different kinds of love. According to Buddhists there are innumerable emotions that are yet to be named in any language, and even more that fall outside of our logical world's ability to define. Some emotions are seemingly rational, but most are irrational. Some seemingly peaceful emotions are rooted in aggression. Some are almost imperceptible. We might think that someone is completely impassive or detached, but that is itself an emotion.

Emotions can be childish. For example, you might get angry because another person is *not* angry and you think they should be. Or you might be upset one day because your partner is too possessive and the next day because she is not possessive enough. Some emotions are amusing to the casual observer, as when Prince Charles, in a clandestine moment of flirtation, remarked to his then mistress Camilla Parker Bowles that he wouldn't mind being reincarnated as her tampon. Some emotions manifest as arrogance, such as the White House–dwellers imposing their idea of liberty on the world. Forcing our personal views on others through strength, blackmail, trickery, or subtle manipulation is also a part of our emotional activity. Not just a few Christians and

Muslims feel passionate about converting heathens to escape hell-fire and damnation, while the existentialists zealously try to convert the religious into heathens. Emotions come in the form of ridiculous pride, as exemplified by Indians who are patriotic toward an India that was shaped by their British oppressors. Many patriotic Americans felt self-righteous emotion when President Bush, from the bridge of the aircraft carrier USS *Abraham Lincoln,* declared victory over Iraq, even though in fact the war had barely begun. Desperation for respect is an emotion: consider Malaysia, Taiwan, and China competing to see who can build the tallest building in the world, as if it were proof of their virility. Emotions can be sick and twisted, leading to pedophilia and bestiality. One man even advertised on the Internet for young men who wanted to be killed and eaten. He received numerous responses, and did indeed kill and devour one of the respondents.

GETTING TO THE ROOT:
THE (NONEXISTENT) SELF

All of these various emotions and their consequences come from misunderstanding, and this misunderstanding comes from one source, which is the root of all ignorance—clinging to the self.

We assume that each of us is a self, that there is an entity called "me." The self is just another misunderstanding, however. We generally manufacture a notion of self, which feels like a solid entity. We are conditioned to view this notion as consistent and real. We think, *I am this form,* raising the hand. We think, *I have form, this is my body.* We think, *Form is me, I am tall.* We think, *I dwell in this form,* pointing at the chest. We do the same with feelings, perceptions, and actions. *I have feelings, I am my perceptions...* But Siddhartha realized that there is no independent entity that qualifies as the self to be found anywhere, either inside or outside the body. Like the optical illusion of a fire ring, the self is illusory.

It is a fallacy, fundamentally flawed and ultimately nonexistent. But just as we can get carried away by the fire ring, we all get carried away by thinking that we are the self. When we look at our own bodies, feelings, perceptions, actions, and consciousness, we see that these are different elements of what we think of as "me," but if we were to examine them, we would find that "me" doesn't dwell in any of them. Clinging to the fallacy of the self is a ridiculous act of ignorance; it perpetuates ignorance; and it leads to all kinds of pain and disappointment. Everything we do in our lives depends on how we perceive our "selves," so if this perception is based on misunderstandings, which it inevitably is, then this misunderstanding permeates everything we do, see, and experience. It is not a simple matter of a child misinterpreting light and movement; our whole existence is based on very flimsy premises.

At the moment that Siddhartha found no self, he also found no inherently existing evil—only ignorance. Specifically, he contemplated the ignorance of creating a label of "self," pasting it on a totally baseless assembled phenomenon, imputing its importance, and agonizing to protect it. This ignorance, he found, leads directly to suffering and pain.

Ignorance is simply not knowing the facts, having the facts wrong, or having incomplete knowledge. All of these forms of ignorance lead to misunderstanding and misinterpretation, overestimation and underestimation. Suppose that you are searching for your friend and you see him in a distant field. When you approach, you discover that you have mistaken a scarecrow for your friend. You are bound to be disappointed. It is not as if either the mischievous scarecrow or your friend tried sneakily to mislead you, it is your own ignorance that betrayed you. Anything we do that emerges from this ignorance is speculative. When we act with no understanding or incomplete understanding, there is no ground for confidence. Our basic insecurity arises and creates all these emotions, named and unnamed, recognized and unrecognized.

The only reason we have to feel confident that we will reach the top of the stairs or that our airplane will take off and land safely at our destination is that we are enjoying the bliss of ignorance. But this bliss doesn't last long, for the bliss of ignorance is nothing more than constant overestimation that the odds of probability will work in our favor, and an underestimation of the obstacles. Of course, causes and conditions do come together and things do happen as we anticipated, but we take this kind of success for granted. We use it as proof that it should not be otherwise, that our assumptions are well-founded. But such assumptions are just food for misunderstanding. Every time we make an assumption—for example, that we understand our spouse—we are exposing ourselves like an open wound. Assumptions and expectations that rely on someone or something else leave us vulnerable. At any moment, one of the uncountable possible contradictions can pop up and sprinkle salt on our assumptions, causing us to flinch and howl.

HABIT: THE SELF'S ALLY

Probably the biggest discovery in human history was Siddhartha's realization that the self does not exist independently, that it is a mere label, and therefore that clinging to it is ignorance. However, as unsound as the label *self* may be, destroying it is no small task. This label called "self" is the most stubborn of all concepts to break.

Siddhartha's discovery of the fallacy of self is symbolized in the story of the destruction of Mara. Referred to traditionally as the evil lord of the desire realm, Mara is none other than Siddhartha's clinging to the self. It is fitting that Mara is depicted as a handsome and powerful warrior who has never been defeated. Like Mara, the self is powerful and insatiable, egocentric and deceptive, greedy for attention, clever, and vain. It's hard to remember that, like the illusion of the fire ring, the self is assembled, doesn't exist independently, and is susceptible to change.

Habit makes us weak against the self. Even simple habits die hard. You may be aware of how bad smoking is for your health, but that doesn't necessarily convince you to stop smoking, especially when you enjoy the ritual, the slender shape of the cigarette, the way the tobacco smolders, the fragrant smoke curling around your fingers. But the habit of self is not just a simple addiction like smoking cigarettes. From time immemorial we have been addicted to the self. It is how we identify ourselves. It is what we love most dearly. It is also what we hate most fiercely at times. Its existence is also the thing that we work hardest to try to validate. Almost everything that we do or think or have, including our spiritual path, is a means to confirm its existence. It is the self that fears failure and longs for success, fears hell and longs for heaven. The self loathes suffering and loves the causes of suffering. It stupidly wages war in the name of peace. It wishes for enlightenment but detests the path to enlightenment. It wishes to work as a socialist but live as a capitalist. When the self feels lonely, it desires friendship. Its possessiveness of those it loves manifests in passion that can lead to aggression. Its supposed enemies—such as spiritual paths designed to conquer the ego—are often corrupted and recruited as the self's ally. Its skill in playing the game of deception is nearly perfect. It weaves a cocoon around itself like a silkworm; but unlike a silkworm, it doesn't know how to find the way out.

WARRING WITH THE SELF

During the battle at Bodh Gaya, Mara deployed a variety of weapons against Siddhartha. In particular, he had a collection of special arrows. Each arrow possessed ruinous powers: the arrow that causes desire, the arrow that causes mental dullness, the arrow that causes pride, the arrow that causes conflict, the arrow that causes arrogance, the arrow that causes blind obsession, and the arrow that causes no awareness, to name a few. In the Buddhist sutras we read that Mara remains undefeated in each of us—he directs his poison arrows at us all the time. When we are hit by Mara's arrows, initially we become numb, but then the poison spreads throughout our being, slowly destroying us. When we lose our awareness and cling to self, it is Mara's numbing poison. Slowly, surely, destructive emotions follow, seeping into our being.

When struck by the desire arrow, all of our common sense, sobriety, and sanity go out the window while false dignity, decadence, and immorality trickle in. Poisoned, we stop at nothing to get what we want. Someone struck with passion might even find a streetwalking hippopotamus sexy, even as a beautiful girl loyally waits for him at home. Like moths to the flame and fish to baited hooks, many on this earth have been ensnared by their desire for food, fame, praise, money, beauty, and respect.

Passion can also manifest as lust for power. Seized with such a passion, leaders are completely indifferent to how their lust for power is destroying the planet. If it were not for certain people's greed for wealth, the highways would be filled with cars powered by the sun, and no one would be starving. Such advances are technologically and physically possible, but apparently not emotionally possible. And meanwhile we grumble about injustice and we blame people like George W. Bush. Struck by the arrows of greed ourselves, we don't see that it is our own desire—to have conveniences like cheap imported electronics and luxuries like Humvees—that actually supports the wars that are devastating our world. Every day during rush hour in Los Angeles, the carpool lane is empty while thousands of cars clog the rest of the road, each with only one occupant. Even those who march in "No Blood for Oil" protests rely on oil to import the kiwifruit for their smoothies.

Mara's arrows create endless conflict. Throughout history, religious figures, those who are supposedly above desire, our models of integrity and propriety, have proved to be equally power hungry. They manipulate their followers with threats of hell and promises of heaven. Today we see politicians manipulating elections and campaigns to the extent that they have no qualms bombarding an innocent country with Tomahawk missiles if it will sway public opinion in their favor. Who cares if you win the war so long as you win the election? Other politicians sanctimoniously flaunt religion, have themselves shot, manufacture heroes, and stage catastrophes, all to satisfy their desire for power.

When the self is full of pride, it manifests in countless ways—narrow-mindedness, racism, fragility, fear of rejection, fear of getting hurt, insensitivity, to name a few. Out of masculine pride, men have stifled the energy and contributions of over half the human race—women. During courtship, each side lets pride get in the way, constantly evaluating whether the other person is good enough for them or whether they are good enough for the other person. Proud families spend fortunes on a one-day wedding ceremony for a marriage that may or may not last, while on the same day, in the same village, people are dying of starvation. A tourist makes a show of giving a ten-dollar tip to the doorman for pushing a revolving door, and the next minute he's bargaining for a five-dollar T-shirt from a vendor who is trying to support her baby and family.

Pride and pity are closely related. Believing that your life is harder and sadder than everyone else's is simply a manifestation of clinging to self. When the self develops self-pity, it eliminates any space that others have to feel compassionate. In this imperfect world so many people have suffered and are still suffering. But some people's suffering has been categorized as a more "special" suffering. Although actual statistics are not available, it seems safe to say that the number of Native Americans slaughtered as

Europeans colonized North America is at least equal to that of other recognized genocides. And yet there is no widely used term—such as *anti-Semitism* or *the Holocaust*—for this inconceivable slaughter.

The mass murders led by Stalin and Mao Tse-tung also don't have recognizable labels, let alone sleek museums, lawsuits for retribution, and endless documentaries and feature films. Muslims cry that they are persecuted, forgetting the destruction wreaked by their Moghul forefathers, who conquered large parts of Asia as missionaries. The evidence of their havoc is still visible—the battered ruins of monuments and temples once created out of love for a different god.

There is also the pride of belonging to a certain school or religion. Christians, Jews, and Muslims all believe in the same God, and in a sense they are brothers. Yet because of the pride of each of these religions and their thinking that they are "right," religion has caused more death than the two world wars put together.

Racism drips from the poisoned arrow of pride. Many Asians and Africans accuse white Westerners of being racist, but racism is also an institution in Asia. At least in the West there are laws against racism, and it is publicly condemned. A Singaporean girl cannot bring her Belgian husband home to meet the family. Ethnic Chinese and Indians in Malaysia cannot have the status of Bhumiputra, even after many generations. Many second-generation Koreans in Japan are still not naturalized. Although many white people adopt children of color, it's unlikely that a well-to-do Asian family would adopt a white child. Many Asians find such cultural and racial intermingling abhorrent. One wonders how the Asians would feel if the tables were turned: if white people had to migrate to China, Korea, Japan, Malaysia, Saudi Arabia, and India by the millions. What if they set up their own communities, took local jobs, imported brides, spoke their own language for generations, refusing to speak the language of the host nation—and on top of that supported religious extremism in their country of origin?

Envy is another of Mara's arrows. It is one of the great loser emotions. It manifests irrationally and generates fantastic stories to distract you. It can strike suddenly at the most unexpected times, perhaps even while you are enjoying yourself at the symphony. Even though you have no intention of becoming a cellist, you have never even touched a cello, you may become jealous of an innocent cello player whom you have never even met. Just the fact that she is talented is enough to poison your mind.

Much of the world is jealous of the United States. Many of the religious and political fanatics who ridicule and criticize the U.S., calling Americans "Satanists" and "imperialists," would fall head over heels for a green card, if they don't already have one. Out of sheer envy, society—often led by the media—almost always topples anyone or anything experiencing success, whether financial, physical, or intellectual. Some journalists purport to defend the underdog and the little people, but often they are afraid to point out that some "underdogs" are really fanatics. These journalists refuse to expose any wrongdoing, and the few who do speak out run the risk of being stigmatized as extremists.

Out of Mara's selfish desire for more disciples, he cleverly preaches freedom, but if someone really exercises freedom, Mara won't necessarily like it. Fundamentally we like to have freedom only for ourselves but not for others. It is no wonder that if we or anyone else really do exercise all our freedoms, we will not be invited to all the parties. This so-called freedom and democracy is just another tool of control by Mara.

WHAT ABOUT LOVE?

One might think that not all emotions are suffering—what about love, joy, creative inspiration, devotion, ecstasy, peace, union, fulfillment, relief? We believe that emotion is necessary for poetry, songs, and art. Our definition of "suffering" isn't fixed, and it is limited. Siddhartha's definition of "suffering" is much more vast and yet much more specific and clear.

Some kinds of suffering, such as aggression, jealousy, and headaches, have an obvious negative quality, while others are more subtly painful. For Siddhartha, anything that has a quality of uncertainty and unpredictability is suffering. For instance, love may be pleasant and fulfilling, but it doesn't spring independently out of the blue. It depends on someone or something, and therefore it is unpredictable. At the very least, one is dependent on the object of love and, in a sense, always on a leash. And the additional hidden conditions are uncountable. For this reason it is also futile to blame our parents for our unhappy childhood or to blame ourselves for our parents' disharmony, because we are not aware of the many hidden dependent conditions involved in these situations.

Tibetans use the words *rangwang* and *shenwang* to represent "happiness" and "unhappiness." They are difficult to translate precisely; *rang* means "self" and *wang* means "power," "rights," or "entitlement," while *shen* means "other." Broadly speaking, as long as one is in control, one is happy, and as long as someone else holds the leash, one is unhappy. Therefore the definition of "happiness" is when one has full control, freedom, rights, leisure, no obstacles, no leash. That means the freedom to choose and the freedom not to choose, the freedom to be active or to be leisurely.

There are certain things we can do to bend conditions to our advantage, such as taking vitamins to become strong or drinking a cup of coffee to wake up. But we can't hold the world still so that it won't stir up another tsunami. We can't prevent a pigeon from hitting the windshield of our car. We can't control the other drivers on the freeway. A big part of our life revolves around trying to make other people cheerful, primarily so that we can feel comfortable. It's not nice living with someone who sulks all the time. But we can't keep another person's emotions upbeat at all times. We can try, and maybe we'll even succeed sometimes, but such manipulation requires a great amount of maintenance. It's not enough to say "I love you" just once in the beginning of a relationship. You have to do the right thing—send flowers, pay attention—until the end. If you fail even once, everything you have built can fall apart. And sometimes, even if you give undivided attention, the object of your attention may misinterpret, not know how to accept, or not be receptive at all. A young man anticipates a candlelight dinner with the girl of his dreams, imagining how the night will unfold, how he will woo and charm her. But that's just his imagination, a guess. Whether it is an educated or an uneducated guess, it's still just a guess. Basically we can't be 100 percent prepared all the time. Therefore our obstacles and opponents need to be successful only 1 percent of the time to do all their damage: a slip of the tongue, accidental expulsion of gas, one casual glance away from the X-ray machine at the airport security checkpoint.

We might think that we aren't really suffering, and even if we are, it isn't so terrible. After all, we aren't living in the gutter or being massacred in Rwanda. Many people think, *I am OK, I am breathing, I am having breakfast, everything is going as well as can be expected, I am not suffering.* But what do they mean? Do they mean this 100 percent? Have they stopped preparing for things to get better? Have they dropped all their insecurities? If such an attitude comes from genuine contentment and appreciation for what they already have, this kind of appreciation is what Siddhartha recommended. But rarely do we ever witness such content; there is always this constant nagging feeling that there is more to life, and this discontent leads to suffering.

Siddhartha's solution was to develop awareness of the emotions. If you can be aware of emotions as they arise, even a little bit, you restrict their activity; they become like teenagers with a chaperone. Someone is watching, and the power of Mara is weakened. Siddhartha was not injured by the poison arrows because of his awareness that they were merely illusions. In the same way, our own powerful emotions can become as harmless as flower petals. And when the apsaras approached Siddhartha, he could see clearly that they were just assembled phenomena, like a fire ring, and therefore they lost their allure. They couldn't get a rise out of him. Similarly, we break the spell of temptation by seeing that the objects of our desire are actually just assembled phenomena.

When you begin to notice the damage that emotions can do, awareness develops. When you have awareness—for example, if you know that you are on the edge of a cliff—you understand the dangers before you. You can still go ahead and do as you were doing; walking on a cliff with awareness is not so frightening anymore, in fact it is thrilling. The real source of fear is not knowing. Awareness doesn't prevent you from living, it makes living that much fuller. If you are enjoying a cup of tea and you understand the bitter and the sweet of temporary things, you will really enjoy the cup of tea.

three

Everything Is Emptiness

*S*oon after Siddhartha's enlightenment, his words, which we call the *dharma*, began to permeate all walks of Indian life. The dharma transcended the caste system and appealed to rich and poor alike. One of the greatest emperors of the third century B.C.E. was King Ashoka, a ruthless warrior and tyrant who had no qualms about murdering his close relatives to consolidate his power. But even King Ashoka eventually found the truth of the dharma and became a pacifist. He is now known as one of Buddhism's most influential historical patrons.

Thanks to patrons like Ashoka, the dharma continued to thrive, traveling in every direction, pulsing far beyond the borders of India. In the first millennium C.E., over six hundred miles from Bodh Gaya, in the Tibetan village of Kya Ngatsa, another ordinary human with extraordinary potential was born. After a hellish childhood and an apprenticeship in black magic, this troubled young man murdered dozens of his family members and neighbors in an act of vengeance. He fled from his home and eventually met a farmer named Marpa, a great dharma teacher and translator who taught the nature of existence and the way of life as it had once been taught by Siddhartha. The young man was transformed. He became known as Milarepa, one of the most renowned yogi saints of Tibet. Even today his songs and stories inspire hundreds of thousands of people. The legacy of his wisdom has been passed down in an unbroken succession of teachers and students.

Milarepa taught his own students that Siddhartha's words are not like other philosophies that we read for pleasure or stimulation and then put on the shelf. We can actually practice the dharma and apply it to our day-to-day life. Among the first generation of Milarepa's students was a brilliant scholar named Rechungpa. Even though Milarepa advised him that integrating practice is more important than mere textbook study, Rechungpa set out for India anyway, intent on receiving classical instruction at one of the great Buddhist philosophical institutions existing at that time. Indeed, Rechungpa studied diligently with many great Indian scholars and saints. When he returned to Tibet after many years, his old master Milarepa came to welcome him on a barren plateau. After they had exchanged greetings and discussed Rechungpa's studies for some time, a violent hailstorm suddenly broke from out of the sky. There was nowhere to hide in the flat open plain. Milarepa spotted a yak horn on the ground and quickly took refuge inside of it—without the horn becoming larger or Milarepa becoming smaller. From his dry shelter, Milarepa sang a song letting Rechungpa know that there was still plenty of space in the yak horn . . . if only his student had realized the nature of emptiness.

You might think that the story of Milarepa's yak horn is merely a fairy tale. Or, if you are the credulous type, you might believe that it was a case of sorcery performed by the Tibetan yogi. But it is neither, as we will see.

GRASPING AT EMPTINESS

By conquering Mara and his army, Siddhartha realized the emptiness of inherent existence. He understood that everything we see, hear, feel, imagine, and know to exist is simply emptiness onto which we have imputed or labeled a certain "trueness." This activity of labeling or perceiving the world as true is born out of a strong individual and collective habit—we all do it. The forces of habit are so strong and our concept of emptiness is so unappealing that few have the will to pursue a realization like Siddhartha's. Instead, we wander like a disoriented desert traveler who sees a lush oasis in the distance. The oasis is actually just the reflection of heat on sand, yet out of desperation, thirst, and hope, the wanderer identifies it as water. Using his last strength to get there, he discovers it is only a mirage and becomes filled with disappointment.

Even though we don't consider ourselves to be so desperate, and believe that we are well educated, sane, and sober, when we see and feel that everything truly exists, we are behaving like the man in the desert. We rush to find authentic companionship, security, recognition, and success, or simply peace and quiet. We may even succeed in grasping some semblance of our desires. But just like the wanderer, when we depend on external substantiation, eventually we are disappointed. Things are not as they seem: they are impermanent and they are not entirely within our control.

If we really analyze, as Siddhartha did, we will find that labels such as "form," "time," "space," "direction," and "size" are easily dismantled. Siddhartha realized that even the self exists only on a relative level, just like a mirage. His realization brought an end to his cycle of expectation, disappointment, and suffering. At the moment of his liberation, he thought, *I have found a path that is profound, peaceful, nonextreme, clear, wish-fulfilling, and nectarlike.*

But if I attempt to express it, if I try to teach, there is no one capable of hearing, listening, or understanding. Therefore I shall remain in this peaceful state in the forest. It is believed that, upon hearing Siddhartha's plans, Lord Indra and Lord Brahma appeared and requested him not to sequester himself in the forest, but to teach for the sake of others. "Even though not everyone will understand all of your teachings," they said, "there are a few who might understand, and to help even those few would be worthwhile."

Respecting their wishes, Siddhartha set out for Varanasi, which even in those days was a great city where intellectuals and thinkers gathered by the river Ganges. When Siddhartha reached Sarnath, which is near Varanasi, he came upon his former colleagues, those who had deserted him long ago when he broke his vows and drank the milk that Sujata offered. When they saw Siddhartha approaching, they quickly conspired to ignore him. They would not greet him, let alone stand up and prostrate to him. "Here comes that phony," they sneered. But for a being who has understood emptiness, as Siddhartha had, notions such as praise and criticism, veneration and contempt, good and bad are utterly inconsequential. They are all a matter of flimsy interpretation, and thus there is no need to react as if they are solid. Therefore Siddhartha approached without a trace of vanity, hesitation, or pride. Because of this lack of self-consciousness, his gait was so majestic that the five meditators had no choice but to stand. Siddhartha delivered his first sermon then and there, with his former colleagues as his first students.

OUR LIMITED LOGIC

Siddhartha was right to think that teaching would be no easy task. In a world that is driven by greed, pride, and materialism, even teaching basic principles such as love, compassion, and philanthropy is very difficult, let alone the ultimate truth of emptiness.

We are stuck with our short-term thinking and bound by practicality. For us, something must be tangible and immediately useful in order to be worth our investment of time and energy. By those criteria, emptiness as defined by Buddha seems completely useless. We might think, *What is the benefit of contemplating the impermanence and emptiness of the phenomenal world? How can emptiness be profitable?*

With our limited rationale, we have a set definition of what makes sense and what is meaningful—and emptiness goes beyond that limit. It is as if the idea of "emptiness" cannot fit inside our heads. This is because the human mind operates on one inadequate system of logic even though there are countless other systems of logic available to us. We operate as if thousands of years of history have preceded this moment, and if someone were to tell us that the entirety of human evolution took place in the duration of a sip of coffee going down the throat, we would not be able to comprehend. Similarly, when we read in Buddhist teachings that one day in hell is equal to five hundred years, we think that these religious figures are just trying to frighten us into submission. But imagine a week's holiday with your best beloved—it goes like the snap of the fingers. On the other hand, one night in prison with a rowdy rapist seems to last forever. Perceived in this way, our concept of time might start to seem not so stable.

Some of us may permit a *little* bit of the unknown into our system of thinking, allowing some space for the possibilities of clairvoyance, intuition, ghosts, soul mates, and so on, but for the most part we rely on black-and-white, scientifically based logic. A small handful of so-called gifted people might have the courage or the skill to go beyond convention, and as long as their view isn't *too* outrageous, they might be able to pass themselves off as artists such as Salvador Dali. There are also a few celebrated yogis who deliberately go just a *little* bit beyond what's conventionally accepted and are venerated as "divine madmen." But if you really go too far beyond the accepted boundary, if you completely buy into emptiness, people may well think that you are abnormal, crazy, and irrational.

But Siddhartha was not irrational. He was merely asserting that conventional, rational thinking is limited. We cannot, or will not, comprehend that which is beyond our own comfort zone. It is much more functional to work with the linear concept of "yesterday, today, and tomorrow" than to say "time is relative." We are not programmed to think, *I can fit into that yak horn without changing my size or shape.* We cannot break our concepts of "small" and "big." Instead we continuously confine ourselves with our safe and narrow perspectives that have been handed down for generations. When these perspectives are examined, however, they don't hold up. For example, the concept of linear time upon which this world relies so heavily does not account for the fact that time has no real beginning and no end.

Using this rationale, which is imprecise at best, we measure or label things as "truly existing." Function, continuity, and consensus play a major part in our process of validation. We think that if something has a function—for example, your hand seems to function by holding this book—then it must exist in a permanent, ultimate, valid sense. A picture of a hand doesn't function in the same way, so we know it isn't really a hand. Similarly, if something seems to have a continuous quality—for example if we saw a mountain yesterday and it is there today—we feel confident that it is "real" and will be there tomorrow and the next day. And when other people confirm that they see the same things we see, we are even more certain that these things are truly existing.

Of course, we don't walk around consciously rationalizing, confirming, and labeling the true existence of things—*this is a truly existing book in my truly existing hands*—but subconsciously we operate in the confidence that the world solidly exists, and this affects how we think and feel every moment of the day. Only on rare occasions, when we look in the mirror or at a mirage, do we appreciate that some things are mere appearances. There is no flesh and blood in the mirror, there is no water in the mirage. We "know" that these mirror images are not real, that they are empty of inherently existing nature. This kind of understanding can take us much further, but we only go as far as our rational mind allows.

When presented with the concept of a man fitting inside of a yak's horn without a change in size, we have a few choices: We can be "rational" and refute the story by saying that it is simply not possible. Or we can apply some kind of mystic belief in sorcery or blind devotion and say, *Oh yes, Milarepa was such a great yogi, of course he could do this and even more.* Either way our view is distorted, because denying is a form of underestimating, and blind faith is a form of overestimating.

YESTERDAY'S RIVER: ACCEPTING PARTIAL LOGIC

Through his tireless contemplation, Siddhartha clearly saw the faults in these conventional forms of estimating, rationalizing, and labeling. Of course they work to an extent—our world seems to function based on these conventions. When we human beings talk about something genuinely and truly existing, we talk about it being definite, not imagined, real, provable, unchanging, and unconditional. Of course, we say that some things change. A bud blooms into a flower, and we still think of it as a truly existing flower as it changes. That growth and change is part of our fixed idea about the nature of the flower. We would be much more surprised if it became permanent. So in that sense, our expectation of change is unchanging.

A river flows with fresh water, always changing, and we still call it a river. If we visit that place a year later, we think it is the same river. But how is it the same? If we isolate one aspect or characteristic, this sameness falls apart. The water is different, the Earth is in a different place in its rotation through the galaxy, the leaves have fallen and been replaced—all that remains is an appearance of a river similar to the one that we saw last time. "Appearance" is quite an unstable basis for "truth." Through simple analysis, the underpinnings of our conventional reality are revealed to be vague generalizations and assumptions. Although Siddhartha used words similar to the ones ordinary people might when defining "truth"—*not imagined, definite, unchanging, unconditional*—his use of these words is much more precise; they are not generalizations. In his view, "unchanging" must mean unchanging in all dimensions, *without exception,* even after thorough analysis.

Our ordinary definition of "truth" is a result of partial analysis. If analysis leads to a comfortable answer, if it gives us what we want, we do not go beyond that. *Is this really a sandwich? It tastes like a sandwich, so I will eat it.* Analysis stops there. A boy is looking for a companion, he sees a girl, she looks beautiful, so he stops analyzing and approaches. Siddhartha's analysis kept going further and further until the sandwich and the girl were just atoms, and finally even the atoms could not hold up to his analysis. Finding nothing there, he was free from disappointment.

Siddhartha found that the only way to confirm something as truly existing is to prove that it exists independently and free of interpretation, fabrication, or change. For Siddhartha, all of the seemingly functional mechanisms of our everyday survival—physical, emotional, and conceptual—fall outside of that definition. They are all put together from unstable, impermanent parts and therefore they are always changing. We can understand this assertion in the conventional world. For example, you could say that your reflection in the mirror does not truly exist because it depends on your standing in front of it. If it were independent, then even without your face, there should be a reflection. Similarly, no thing can truly exist without depending on so many uncountable conditions.

We look at a fire ring and we have no problem understanding the conditions of its fabrication. We accept that as long as these parts are all working together, it is really a fire ring . . . for now. But why can't we think that way about the book we are holding or the bed we are lying on? It looks like a book, other people see it as a book, it functions like a book; but when you analyze it, the "for now" principle can be applied to it as well. Everything we perceive during our lives is "for now." Things appear to exist for the moment; we just don't have the courage or the will to look at it this way. And because we don't have the intelligence to see things in parts, we settle for looking at them as a whole. If all the feathers are plucked from a peacock, we are no longer awed by it. But we are not eager to surrender to seeing all the world this way. It's like being curled up in bed having a good dream, slightly conscious that you are dreaming, and not wanting to wake up. Or seeing a beautiful rainbow and not wanting to get close because it will disappear. Having the courageous spirit to wake up and examine is what Buddhists call "renunciation." Contrary to popular belief, Buddhist renunciation is not self-flagellation or austerity. Siddhartha was willing and able to see that all of our existence is merely labels placed on phenomena that do not truly exist, and through that he experienced awakening.

BUDDHA WAS NOT A MASOCHIST

Many people who have only a vague idea of what Buddha taught think that Buddhism is morbid, that Buddhists negate happiness and think only of suffering. They assume that Buddhists shun beauty and physical enjoyments because they are temptations; Buddhists are supposed to be pure and temperate.

Actually Siddhartha's teachings are not prejudiced against beauty and enjoyment any more than they're against other concepts—as long as we don't get carried away into thinking that such things really exist.

Siddhartha had a lay disciple, a warrior named Manjushri, who was known as a great wit and a trickster. Among Manjushri's fellow students was a very diligent and respected monk who was well-known for his "ugliness meditation," a method that is prescribed, among many others, to those who are desire-oriented and have a lot of passion. It involves imagining all human beings as made of veins, cartilage, intestines, and such. Manjushri decided to test the diligent monk by using his supernatural powers. He transformed himself into a beautiful nymph and appeared before the monk to seduce him. For some time the good monk remained uncorrupted, not moving a muscle. But Manjushri proved to be overpoweringly seductive, and the monk began to fall under his spell. He was surprised because during many years of meditation he had successfully resisted some of the most beautiful women in the land. Shocked and disappointed in himself, the monk fled. But the nymph Manjushri chased him until the exhausted monk collapsed on the ground. As the seductive woman approached him, he thought, *That's it, this beautiful girl is about to embrace me.* He shut his eyes tightly and waited, but nothing happened. When he finally opened his eyes, the nymph had been dismantled into fragments and Manjushri appeared, laughing. "Thinking that someone is beautiful is a concept," he said. "Clinging to that concept confines you, ties you in a knot, and imprisons you. But if you think that someone is ugly, that is also a concept, and that will also bind you."

Every year we spend huge sums of money making ourselves and our environment attractive. But what is beauty? We may say that it is in the eye of the beholder, yet millions of us tune in to the Miss Universe Pageant to be told who is the most beautiful in all the universe, according to a panel of judges. These ten or so people allegedly give us the ultimate definition of beauty. Of course there will always be dissenters, given the fact that within this universe they are ignoring the beautiful women of Papua New Guinea and the elegant African tribal women who wear rings around their elongated necks.

If Siddhartha sat in on a Miss Universe Pageant, he would see another kind of ultimate beauty altogether. To his eyes, the one who is crowned cannot be the ultimate beauty because her beauty depends on the beholder. Because Siddhartha's definition of "ultimate" requires independence from any and all conditions, for her to be truly beautiful, there would be no need for the condition of a pageant because everyone would automatically agree that she is the ultimate. And if she is truly beautiful, there cannot be a moment of being slightly not-so-beautiful. She would have to be beautiful when she's yawning, when she's snoring, when saliva is dripping from her mouth, when she's squatting on the toilet, when she's old—*all* the time.

Instead of seeing one contestant as any more or less beautiful than the others, Siddhartha would see that all women are empty of both ugliness and beauty. The beauty he sees is in the hundreds of millions of perspectives from which any one contestant can be viewed. Of the abundant points of view in the universe, someone must be jealous, someone must see her as their lover, their daughter, sister, mother, friend, rival. To a crocodile she is food, to a parasite she is a host. To Siddhartha, this array is in itself astonishingly beautiful, whereas if someone is truly and ultimately beautiful, she would have to be fixed in that state of beauty forevermore. All the gowns and swimsuits, lights and lipstick would not be necessary. As it is, we have the display of the pageant and *for now,* the spectacle is as beautiful as our old assembled and impermanent fire ring.

RELATIVE TRUTH: EXISTING "SOMEWHAT"

In Buddhist philosophy, anything that is perceived by the mind did not exist before the mind perceived it; it depends on the mind. It doesn't exist independently, therefore it doesn't truly exist. That is not to say that it doesn't exist *somewhat*. Buddhists call the perceived world "relative" truth—a truth that is measured and labeled by our ordinary minds. In order to qualify as "ultimate" truth, it must not be fabricated, it must not be a product of the imagination, and it must be independent of interpretation.

Although Siddhartha realized emptiness, emptiness was not manufactured by Siddhartha or anyone else. Emptiness is not the result of his revelation, nor was it developed as a theory to help people be happy. Whether or not Siddhartha taught it, emptiness has always been emptiness, although paradoxically we can't even really say that emptiness has always been, because it is beyond time and has no form. Nor should emptiness be interpreted as negation of existence—that is, we can't say that this relative world doesn't exist either—because in order to negate something, you have to acknowledge that there is something to negate in the first place. Emptiness doesn't cancel out our daily experience. Siddhartha never said that something spectacular, better, purer, or more divine exists in place of what we perceive. He wasn't an anarchist refuting the appearance or function of worldly existence, either. He didn't say that there is no appearance of a rainbow or that there is no cup of tea. We can enjoy our experience, but just because we can experience something doesn't mean that it truly exists. Siddhartha simply suggested that we examine our experience and consider that it could be just a temporary illusion, like a daydream.

If someone asked you to flap your arms and fly, you would say, "I can't," because in our experience of the relative world it is not physically possible to fly, any more than it is possible to hide inside a yak horn. But suppose that you are asleep and dreaming that you are flying through the sky. If someone in the dream says, "Human beings can't fly," you will say, "Yes, I can—see?" And you will fly away. Siddhartha would agree on both counts— you *can't* fly when you are awake, and you *can* fly when you are asleep. The reasons are the causes and conditions that have or have not come together; a condition necessary to be able to fly is to be dreaming. When it is not there, you can't fly, when it is you can. If you dream that you are flying and continue to believe that you can fly even after you wake up, that becomes a problem. You will fall and you will be disappointed. Siddhartha says that even when we wake up in the relative world, we are asleep with igno- rance, like the palace courtesans on the night that he fled his pre- vious existence. When the right causes and conditions come together, anything can appear. But when those conditions are ex- hausted, the appearance stops.

Viewing our experience in this world as a dream, Siddhartha found that our habit of fixating on the mere appearance of our dreamlike relative world, thinking that it is truly existing, throws us into an endless cycle of pain and anxiety. We are in a deep sleep, hibernating like a silkworm in a cocoon. We have woven a reality based on our projections, imagination, hopes, fears, and delu- sions. Our cocoons have become very solid and sophisticated. Our imaginings are so real to us that we are trapped in the cocoon. But we can free ourselves simply by realizing that this is all our imagination.

There must be infinite ways to wake up from this sleep. Even substances like peyote and mescaline might give us a vague notion of the illusory aspect of "reality." But a drug cannot pro- vide total awakening, if only because this awakening is dependent on an external substance and when the effect of the mescaline is gone, the experience is gone as well. Suppose that you are having a really bad dream. All it takes is a flicker of realization that you are dreaming to wake you up. The spark can come from within a dream. When you do something anomalous within the dream, you may be jostled into realizing that you are asleep. Peyote and mescaline can spark a short-lived realization by revealing the power of the mind and the imagination. Hallucinations help us temporarily recognize how tangible and believable illusions can be. But such substances are not advisable because they provide only an artificial experience, one that can actually harm the body. Instead we should have the aspiration to wake up once and for all, without depending on external input. We are much better off when realization comes from within. What we really need is to wake up from our habitual patterns, imagination, and greed. Mind training and meditation are the swiftest, safest, and most effective ways to work within the mindstream. As Siddhartha said, "You are your own master."

"IT IS THE ATTACHMENT THAT BINDS YOU"

Siddhartha completely understood that in the relative world you can make a cup of oolong tea and drink it; he would not say, "There is no tea" or "Tea is emptiness." If he were to say anything at all, it would be to suggest that the tea is not as it seems; for example, tea is shriveled leaves in hot water. But some tea fanatics get carried away with the leaves and composing special mixes, creating names like Iron Dragon and selling small amounts for hundreds of dollars. To them it is not just a leaf in water. It was for this reason that some fifteen hundred years after Siddhartha taught, one of his dharma heirs, named Tilopa, said to his student, Naropa, "It is not the appearance that binds you, it's the attachment to the appearance that binds you."

There was once a beautiful nun called Utpala. A man fell deeply in love with her and began to stalk her. His pursuit made her uncomfortable, and she tried to avoid him, but he was relentless. Finally one day, to his complete shock, she came toward him and confronted him. Fumbling for words, he blurted out that he loved her eyes. Without hesitation she took them out and handed them to him. His shock made him see how easily one is caught up and obsessed with assembled parts. When he overcame his shock and horror, he became her disciple.

In another Japanese Buddhist fable, two traveling Zen monks were about to wade across a river when a young woman asked them to carry her over the swift water. Both of these monks had taken advanced vows and were not permitted to touch women, but without hesitation the older monk lifted her up, put her on his back, and walked across. When they reached the other side, he let the woman down and, without any small talk, walked away. A few hours later the younger monk blurted out, "Aren't we monks? Why did you carry that woman?"

The older monk replied, "I put her down a long time ago. Why are you still carrying her?"

In a moment of clarity we may be able to see the emptiness of abstract concepts such as beauty and ugliness—they are open to interpretation, after all—but it is much more difficult for us to understand the emptiness of nonabstract things such as the car that needs repair, the bills that must be paid, the health-threatening high blood pressure, the family that supports us or that needs our support. It's understandable that we aren't willing or able to see these things as illusory. It's much more ridiculous when we get caught up in extravagances such as high fashion, haute cuisine, celebrity status, and membership in elite clubs. More than a few people are so spoiled that having a television in every room or two hundred pairs of shoes seems like a necessity. Lusting after a pair of Nikes or a Giorgio Armani suit at a posh boutique goes far beyond the practical survival impulse. People even get into fights over handbags in stores. The assembled phenomena of packaging and market research are so intricate and calculated that we become suckers for labels, accepting the ridiculous price tags that have no correlation with material value.

Since the majority of people subscribe to the point of view that these things have value, it's difficult for an image-conscious Louis Vuitton–lover to understand the essenceless of her obsession with her genuine leather handbag, let alone the essenceless of the bag itself. Reinforced by popular culture, the importance of bourgeois status and labels becomes more solid in our minds, making our world ever more artificial.

On top of being manipulated by bill collectors and marketing geniuses, we are pushed and pulled by political systems such as democracy and communism, abstract concepts such as individual rights, and moral positions such as antiabortion and "the right to die." The political world is filled with such labels, and the chances of genuine leadership are slim to none. Human beings have experimented with various types of leadership, and each of them has its benefits, yet many people still suffer. There may be some politicians with real integrity, but in order to win an election, they must label themselves as pro–gay rights or anti–gay rights, even if they don't have strong feelings on the issue. Most often we find ourselves unwillingly complying with what the majority thinks, even if it is an insane position, in order to get along in this so-called democratic world.

A long time ago, in a drought-ridden country, a respected soothsayer predicted that after seven days there would finally be rain. His prediction came true and there was great rejoicing. He then predicted a rain of jewels, and once again his prediction was accurate. The people were very happy and prosperous. His next prediction was that after seven days there would be another rain, a cursed rain, and anyone who drank this rainwater would go insane. The king ordered huge amounts of uncontaminated water to be stored so that he wouldn't have to drink the cursed rain. But his subjects didn't have the resources to store their water. When the rain came, they drank the water and became crazy. The king alone was "sane," but he could not rule his crazy subjects, so as a last resort he, too, drank the water. In order to rule them, he needed to share in their delusions.

As in the Miss Universe contest, everything that we do or think in this world is based on a very limited system of shared logic. We put so much emphasis on consensus. If the majority agrees that something is true, then it usually becomes valid. When we look at a small pond, we humans just see a pond; but to the fish in the pond this is their universe. If we take a democratic stance, then the aquatic dwellers should win because there are many more of them than there are of us pond gazers. Majority rule doesn't always work. Terrible blockbuster films can gross huge profits, while a fascinating independent film is seen by only a handful of people. And because of our reliance on group thinking, the world is often ruled by the most shortsighted and corrupt rulers; democracy appeals to the lowest common denominator.

THE TRUTH: NOT A FABLE, NOT MAGIC, NOT DEADLY

It is difficult for us whose minds are conditioned by pragmatism to understand emptiness; that's why Milarepa's refuge inside the yak horn is almost always brushed aside as a fable. It cannot fit inside our small brain, just as the ocean cannot fit inside a well. Once there was a frog who lived in a well. One day he met a frog from the ocean. The ocean frog told fantastic tales of his ocean and boasted of its vastness. But the well frog couldn't believe him; he believed his well to be the biggest and most fabulous body of water in the world because he had no reference point, no experience, no reason to think otherwise. So the ocean frog took the well frog to the ocean. Facing the vastness of the ocean, the well frog died of a heart attack.

Realization isn't necessarily lethal. We don't have to be like the well frog, dropping dead when we are exposed to emptiness. If the ocean frog had been a bit more compassionate and skillful, he might have been a better guide, and the well frog wouldn't have died. Perhaps he would have eventually migrated to the ocean. We don't need a supernatural gift to understand emptiness. It's a matter of education and a willingness to see things in terms of all their parts and hidden causes and conditions. With such insight, one becomes like a set designer or a camera assistant who goes to the cinema. Professionals see beyond what we see. They see how the camera was positioned, which lenses and lighting equipment were used, how the crowds were computer generated, and all the other cinematic techniques that the audience isn't aware of, and thus for them the illusion is dismantled. Yet the professionals can still enjoy themselves immensely when they go to the cinema. This is an example of Siddhartha's transcendent humor.

NECKTIES AND THE NOOSE OF EMOTION

The classic Buddhist example used to illustrate emptiness is the snake and the rope. Let's say there is a cowardly man named Jack who has a phobia about snakes. Jack walks into a dimly lit room, sees a snake coiled up in the corner, and panics. In fact he is looking at a striped Giorgio Armani tie, but in his terror he has misinterpreted what he sees to the point that he could even die of fright—death caused by a snake that does not truly exist. While he is under the impression that it is a snake, the pain and anxiety that he experiences is what Buddhists call "samsara," which is a kind of mental trap. Fortunately for Jack, his friend Jill walks into the room. Jill is calm and sane and knows that Jack thinks he sees a snake. She can switch on the light and explain that there is no snake, that it is actually a tie. When Jack is convinced that he is safe, this relief is none other than what Buddhists call "nirvana"—

liberation and freedom. But Jack's relief is based on a fallacy of harm being averted, even though there was no snake and there was nothing to cause his suffering in the first place.

It's important to understand that by switching on the light and demonstrating that there is no snake, Jill is also saying that there is no absence of the snake. In other words, she cannot say, "The snake is gone now," because the snake was never there. She didn't make the snake disappear, just as Siddhartha didn't make emptiness. This is why Siddhartha insisted that he could not sweep away the suffering of others by waving his hand. Nor could his own liberation be granted or shared piecemeal, like some sort of award. All he could do was explain from his experience that there was no suffering in the first place, which is like switching on the light for us.

When Jill finds Jack frozen in terror, she has some choices about what to do. She can directly point out that there is no snake, or she can use a skillful method such as escorting the "snake" from the room. But if Jack is so terrified that he is unable to differentiate the snake from the tie, even with the light on, and if Jill is not skillful, then she could actually make things worse. If she dangles the necktie in Jack's face, he could die of a heart attack. But if Jill is skillful and sees that Jack is delusional, she can say, "Yes, I see the snake," and carefully take the tie out of the room so that Jack feels safe for the time being. Maybe then, when he is relaxed, he can be gently guided to the point of seeing that there was never a snake in the first place.

If Jack had never even gone into the room, if there was no misapprehension, then the whole scenario of seeing a snake or not seeing a snake is nullified. But because he saw a snake and is caught in the scenario, and because he is paralyzed with fear, he wants a means of escape. Siddhartha's teachings are a method for such liberation. The dharma is sometimes referred to as a "holy" path, although strictly speaking there is no divinity in Buddhism.

A path is a method or a tool that leads us from one place to another; in this case, the path leads us out of ignorance to the absence of ignorance. We use the word *holy* or *venerable* because the wisdom of dharma can release us from fear and suffering, which is generally the role of the divine.

Our everyday experience of life is full of uncertainties, occasional joys, anxieties, and emotions that coil around us like a snake. Our hopes, fears, ambitions, and general hysteria create the darkness and shadows that allow the illusion of the snake to become even more vivid. Like the cowardly Jack, we hunt for solutions in all corners of the darkened room. The sole purpose of Siddhartha's teaching is to help cowards like us understand that our suffering and paranoia are all based on illusions.

Even though Siddhartha could not erase suffering with the wave of a wand or some divine power, he was very skillful when it came to switching on the light. He provided many paths and methods for discovering the truth. In fact there are tens of thousands of paths to follow within Buddhism. So why not simplify it into one method? The reason is that, like the variety of medicines needed for different diseases, a variety of methods are necessary for different kinds of habits, cultures, and attitudes. Whichever one is followed depends on the state of mind of the student and the skill with which the teacher is adorned. Instead of shocking everyone with emptiness right from the beginning, Siddhartha taught his masses of students with popular methods such as meditation and codes of conduct—"Do the right thing, don't steal, don't tell lies." He prescribed different levels of renunciation and austerity, from shaving heads to abstaining from meat, depending on the nature of the student. Seemingly religious and strict paths work well for those who cannot initially hear or comprehend emptiness, as well as for those whose nature is suited to asceticism.

HOW BUDDHA TAUGHT: DHARMA AS PLACEBO

Some people think that stringent rules and virtuous deeds are the essence of Buddhism, but these are only a small component of Buddha's skillful and abundant methods. He knew that not everyone is able to understand ultimate truths right from the start. It is difficult for many of us to process concepts such as "hell is merely the perception of your own aggression," let alone the concept of emptiness. Buddha doesn't want Jack to be caught in a personal "hell," but he can't tell Jack to work with his perceptions and aggression either because Jack is an idiot. So for Jack's sake, Buddha teaches that there is an external hell and that in order to avoid going there and being boiled in molten iron, Jack must stop entertaining his nonvirtuous, negative actions and emotions. Such teachings pervade the Buddhist milieu; very often we see hell realms painted on the walls of Buddhist temples, complete with burning bodies and terrifying gorges of frigid water. These images can be taken literally or figuratively, depending on the capacity of the student. Those with superior faculties know that the source of our everyday hell, our suffering, stems from our own perceptions. They know that there is no judgment day and there is no judge. When Milarepa appeared in the yak horn, Rechungpa was on his way to becoming a great master himself. He had an enormous capacity to understand emptiness intellectually and enough realization to actually *see* Milarepa in the yak horn; but his realization stopped just short of being able to join his master. Buddha's final aim is to make Jack understand, like these superior students, that there is no hell realm apart from his own aggression and ignorance. By temporarily minimizing his negative actions, Jack is diverted from becoming more entangled with his perceptions, misgivings, and paranoia.

. . .

The word *karma* is practically synonymous with Buddhism. It is usually understood as a sort of moralistic system of retribution—"bad" karma and "good" karma. But karma is simply a law of cause and effect, not to be confused with morality or ethics. No one, including Buddha, set the fundamental bar for what is negative and what is positive. Any motivation and action that steer us away from such truths as "all compounded things are impermanent" can result in negative consequences, or bad karma. And any action that brings us closer to understanding such truths as "all emotions are pain" can result in positive consequences, or good karma. At the end of the day, it was not for Buddha to judge; only you can truly know the motivation behind your actions.

In a discussion with his disciple Subhuti, Siddhartha said, "Those who see Buddha as a form and those who hear Buddha as a sound have the wrong view." Four hundred years later the great Indian Buddhist scholar Nagarjuna concurred. In his famous treatise on Buddhist philosophy, he devoted an entire chapter to "Analyzing the Buddha," and concluded that ultimately there is no externally existing buddha. Even today, it is not unusual to hear Buddhist sayings such as, "If you see buddha on the road, kill him." This is of course meant figuratively; certainly one should not kill him. It means that the real buddha is not an externally existing savior bound by time and space. On the other hand, a man named Siddhartha did appear on this earth who became known as Gautama Buddha and walked barefoot on the streets of Magadha begging alms. This buddha gave sermons, nursed the sick, and even visited his family in Kapilavastu. The reason Buddhists will not dispute that this physical buddha existed in the fifth century B.C.E. in India—as opposed to modern-day Croatia, for example—is that we have historical records that for centuries he has served as a source of inspiration in India. He was a great teacher, the first in a long line of learned masters and disciples. It is nothing more than that. Yet for a serious seeker, inspiration is everything.

Siddhartha used many skillful methods to inspire people. One day a monk noticed a tear in Gautama Buddha's robe and offered to stitch it, but Buddha refused his offer. He kept walking and begging alms in his torn robe. When he headed toward the hideout of a destitute woman, the monks were puzzled because they knew that she had no alms to offer. When she saw his torn robe, the woman offered to mend it with what little string she had. Siddhartha accepted and declared that her virtue would allow her to be reborn in her next life as a queen of the heavens. Many people who heard this story were inspired to acts of generosity of their own.

In another story, Siddhartha cautioned a butcher that killing generated negative karma. But the butcher said, "This is all I know, it is my livelihood." Siddhartha told the butcher to at least take a vow not to kill from sunset to sunrise. He was not giving permission for the butcher to kill during the daytime, but was guiding him to gradually minimize his unwholesome actions. These are examples of the skillful means that Buddha employed to teach the dharma. He was not saying that because the poor woman stitched *his* robe, she was going to heaven, as if he were divine. It was her own generosity that caused her good fortune.

You might think that this is a paradox. Buddha contradicts himself, saying that he doesn't exist, that everything is emptiness, and then teaching morality and salvation. But these methods are necessary in order not to scare people who are not ready to be introduced to emptiness. They are pacified and made ready for the real teachings. It is like saying that there *is* a snake and throwing the tie out the window. These infinite methods are the path. However, the path itself must eventually be abandoned, just as you abandon a boat when you reach the other shore. You must disembark once you have arrived. At the point of total realization, you must abandon Buddhism. The spiritual path is a temporary solution, a placebo to be used until emptiness is understood.

THE BENEFITS OF UNDERSTANDING

You may still ponder, *What is the benefit of understanding emptiness?* By understanding emptiness, you maintain an appreciation for all that appears to exist, but without clinging to the illusions as if they were real and without the incessant disappointment of a child chasing a rainbow. You see through the illusions and are reminded that it is the self that created them in the first place. You may still get stirred up or emotional, sad, angry, or passionate, but you have the confidence of someone at the cinema who can leave the drama behind because there is a clear understanding that it is just a movie. Your hopes and fears are at least slightly diffused, like recognizing that the snake is just a tie.

When we have not realized emptiness, when we don't fully understand that all things are illusions, the world seems real, tangible, and solid. Our hopes and fears also become solid and thus uncontrollable. For example, if you have a solid belief in your family, you have a deep-seated expectation that your parents will take care of you. You don't feel that way about a stranger on the street; he has no such obligation. Understanding assembled phenomena and understanding emptiness allow for some room in the relationship. As you begin to see the various experiences, pressures, and circumstances that molded your parents, your expectations of them change, your disappointment lessens. When some of us become parents ourselves, even a little understanding of interdependence effectively softens our expectations of our children, which they may interpret as love. Without that understanding, we might have good intentions to love and care for our children, but our expectations and demands can become unbearable.

Similarly, by understanding emptiness, you lose interest in all the trappings and beliefs that society builds up and tears down—political systems, science and technology, global economy, free society, the United Nations. You become like an adult who is not so interested in children's games. For so many years you have trusted these institutions and believed that they could succeed where past systems have failed. But the world has not yet become safer, more pleasant, securer.

This is not to say that you should drop out of society. Having an understanding of emptiness doesn't mean that you become blasé; to the contrary, you develop a feeling of responsibility and compassion. If Jack is howling, making a scene, yelling at everyone to stop putting snakes in the house, and you know it is because of his delusion, you have sympathy for him. Others may not be so forgiving, so you can try turning on some lights, for Jack's sake. On a gross level, you will still fight for your individual rights, hold down a job, be politically active within the system; but when the situation changes, either for or against you, you are prepared. You don't blindly believe that everything you wish for and expect must materialize, and you're not caught up in the end result.

More often than not, many of us choose to stay in the dark. We aren't able to see the illusions that create our everyday life because we don't have the courage to break out of the network that we're plugged in to. We think that we are, or will soon be, comfortable enough if we continue on as we are going. It's as if we are entering a maze through which we already have a habitual route, and we don't want to explore other directions. We are not adventurous because we think we have so much to lose. We fear that if we see the world from the view of emptiness, we may be cast out from society, lose our respectability and along with it our friends, family, and job. The seductive allure of the illusory world doesn't help; it's packaged so well. We are bombarded with messages about soap that makes us smell like heaven, how miraculous the South Beach Diet is, how democracy is the only viable system of government, how vitamins will increase our stamina. We rarely hear more than one side of the truth, and on the rare occasions that we do, it's usually in fine print. Imagine George W. Bush going to Iraq and proclaiming, *American-style democracy might or might not work in your country*.

Like a child at the cinema, we get caught up in the illusion. From this comes all of our vanity, ambition, and insecurity. We fall in love with the illusions we have created and develop excessive pride in our appearance, our possessions, and our accomplishments. It's like wearing a mask and proudly thinking that the mask is really you.

Once there were five hundred monkeys, one of whom thought he was very clever. One night this monkey saw the reflection of the moon in the lake. He proudly informed all the other monkeys, "If we go to the lake and collect the moon, then we will be the heroes who saved the moon." At first the other monkeys didn't believe him. But when they saw with their own eyes that the moon had fallen into the lake, they decided to try to save it. They climbed a tree and held each other by the tail so they could reach the shimmering moon. Just as the last monkey was about to grab the moon, the branch broke and they all fell in the lake. They didn't know how to swim and they all struggled in the water as the image of the moon shattered in the ripples. Driven by the hunger for fame and originality, we are like these monkeys, thinking that we are so clever in discovering things and convincing our fellow humans to see what we see, think what we think, driven by ambition to be the savior, the clever one, the seer of all. We have all kinds of small ambitions, such as impressing a girl, or big ambitions, such as landing on Mars. And time after time we end up in the water with nothing to hold on to and not knowing how to swim.

. . .

Having understood emptiness, Siddhartha had no preference whether he lay on the kusha grass beneath the bodhi tree or on the silk cushions in the palace. The higher value placed on golden-threaded cushions is completely fabricated by human ambition and desire. In fact, a mountain hermit might find the kusha grass more soothing and clean, and best of all, if it gets worn out, there is no worry. You don't have to spray it with repellent to prevent your cats from digging their claws into it. Palace life is filled with such "precious items" that require maintenance. But if forced to make a choice, Siddhartha would choose the grass mats so he wouldn't have much to maintain.

We humans consider broad-mindedness to be a virtue. In order to broaden our minds, it is important not to settle merely for what makes us comfortable and what we are used to. It helps if we have the courage to go beyond the norms and not get stuck within the usual boundaries of logic. If we can go beyond the boundaries, we will realize that emptiness is ridiculously simple. Milarepa taking shelter inside the yak horn will be no more surprising than someone putting on a pair of gloves. The challenge lies in our attachment to using the same old logic, grammar, alphabet, and numerical equations. If we can remember the compounded nature of these habits, we can cut through them. They are not impossible to break. All it takes is one situation when the conditions are precisely right and one piece of timely information is provided; then you may suddenly realize that all the tools you rely on are not so rigid—they are elastic, bendable. Your point of view will change. If someone you trust tells you that the wife that you have been resenting all these years is actually a goddess of wealth in disguise, then how you look at her will change in every way. Similarly, if you are enjoying a delicious steak with all kinds of sauces at a nice restaurant, savoring every bite, and then the chef tells you it is actually human flesh, instantly the experience changes 180 degrees. Your concept of delicious becomes a concept of revolting.

When you wake up from a dream about five hundred elephants, you aren't puzzled about how the elephants were able to fit into your room because they didn't exist before, during, or after the dream. Yet when you were dreaming about them, they were perfectly real. One day we will realize, not just intellectually, that there is no such thing as "big" and "small," "gain" or "loss," that it is all relative. Then we will be able to understand how Milarepa fit inside the yak horn and why a tyrant like King Ashoka bowed down and submitted to this truth.

four

~~~~

Nirvana Is beyond Concepts

According to Buddhists, before this life in which he attained enlightenment, Siddhartha lived countless lives as birds, monkeys, elephants, kings, queens, and many as a bodhisattva, a being whose sole aim is to overcome ignorance in order to benefit all beings. But it was in his lifetime as the Indian prince Siddhartha that he at long last defeated Mara beneath the bodhi tree and finally reached the other shore, the other side of samsara. This state is referred to as "nirvana." Having reached nirvana, he gave his first sermon in Sarnath, near Varanasi, and continued to teach throughout northern India for the rest of his long life. His students were monks and nuns, kings and warlords, courtesans and merchants. Many members of his family became renunciants, including his wife, Yashodhara, and his son, Rahula. He was venerated as a supreme human by many people from all over India and beyond. But he did not become immortal. After a long life of teaching, he passed away in a place called Kushinagar. At that moment he went even beyond nirvana to a state that is called "parinirvana."

HEAVEN: THE ULTIMATE VACATION?

Nirvana, enlightenment, liberation, freedom, heaven—these are words that many people like to utter and few have time to examine. How would it be to enter into one of these states? Even though we may think that nirvana is far different from heaven, our versions of heaven and nirvana have roughly the same characteristics. Heaven/nirvana is where we go when we die after many years of paying dues, doing practice, and being good citizens. We will meet many of our old comrades because it is a place where all the "good" dead people gather, while all the not-so-good dead people suffer down below. We finally have a chance to solve life's mysteries, finish unfinished business, make amends, and maybe see into our past lives. Small babies without sex organs fly around doing our ironing. Our dwelling meets our every need and desire and is well situated in a community of other nirvana-dwellers who obey the rules. We never have to lock the windows and doors, and there is probably no need for police. If there are politicians, they are all reliable and honest. Everything is exactly to our liking; it's like a very pleasant retirement home. Or perhaps some of us imagine the purest of pure white light, spaciousness, rainbows, and clouds upon which we rest in a blissful state practicing our powers of clairvoyance and omniscience. There is no death to fear because you are already dead and there is nothing to lose. The only concern we might have is worrying about some of our dear friends and family members whom we've left behind.

Siddhartha found these versions of the afterlife to be fantasies. Under close scrutiny, the typical vision of heaven is not that attractive, and neither is enlightenment. Retirement, honeymoons, and picnics are pleasing—but not if they're infinite. If our dream vacation lasts too long, we become nostalgic for home. If the perfect life contains no knowledge of suffering or risk, it can be boring. The moment you have the knowledge that these things exist, you have a choice—to be either condescending or filled with empathy toward those who suffer. That is not heavenly. Here in the mundane world we can watch detective movies, thrillers, and erotic films. In heaven you can't enjoy suggestive language or provocative clothing because if you are omniscient, you know what is behind it all. We can celebrate Friday night after a hard week at work. We can enjoy the change of seasons and install the latest software on our computers. We can open up the morning paper, read about all the unfortunate things happening in the world, and fantasize about what we would do if we could swap places with world leaders. All this, despite the fact that many of our "simple pleasures" are really problems, not even in disguise. If you like watching football with a beer in your hand, then you are bound to watching the game for a full two hours and are not so free to do other things, you are vulnerable to interruptions, you must pay for the cable hookup and the groceries, your cholesterol may go up, and you are at risk of having heart failure if the other team scores.

By contrast, the enlightenment that we imagine is an unchanging problem-free zone. Can we handle a state where there are no obstacles? We would have to do without many of the thrills, achievements, and entertainments that we believe constitute our happiness. Surely Eminem fans would get sick of all the harp music in heaven—they would want to hear his latest album with all its offensive language. If we accept enlightenment as we've imagined it, we wouldn't be able to enjoy suspense films; our power of omniscience would ruin the surprise ending. There would be no more excitement at the racetrack because we would already know the winning horse.

Immortality is another attribute commonly assigned to enlightenment or heaven. Once we arrive at our new home in the clouds, we will never die again, so we have no choice but to live on forever. We are stuck. There is no escape. We have everything we ever dreamed of except a way out, surprises, challenges, satisfactions—and free will, because we don't need it anymore. Taking all this into consideration, from our present point of view, enlightenment is the ultimate state of boredom.

But most of us don't critically examine our version of an afterlife; we prefer to keep it vague, with a general sense that it is a good final resting place. The enlightenment we long for is forever, a sort of permanent residence. Or some may think that they can come back for a visit as a sort of deity or higher being possessing special powers we mortals don't have. They would have angelic immunity, like a diplomat traveling on a special passport. And because of their immunity and high ranking, they think they will be able to arrange visas and shepherd their loved ones back with them. But then the question arises, if some of these new immigrants have their own set way of thinking—perhaps they like to wear certain conspicuous socks that distract other heavenly beings—won't heaven have a problem? And if all the "good people" are given membership to heaven or nirvana, whose version of happiness prevails?

No matter how we define it, the ultimate goal of every being is happiness. It's no wonder that happiness is an indispensable part of the definition of heaven or enlightenment. A good afterlife should include finally getting what we have always strived for. Generally, in our personal version of heaven we live in a system that is similar to our current system, except that it's more sophisticated and things work better.

HAPPINESS IS NOT THE GOAL

Most of us believe that the ultimate achievement on the spiritual path comes only after this life is over. We are stuck with these impure surroundings and bodies, therefore we must die in order to fully succeed. Only after death will we experience the divine or enlightened state. So the best thing we can do in this life is prepare for it; what we do now will determine whether we go to heaven or to hell. Some people have already lost hope. They feel that they are inherently bad or evil, and don't deserve to go to heaven— they are predestined for the netherworld. Similarly, many Buddhists know intellectually that everyone has the same potential and the same nature as Gautama Buddha, yet emotionally they feel that they don't have the qualities or abilities to gain access to the golden gates of enlightenment. At least not in this life.

For Siddhartha the ultimate resting place of heaven or nirvana isn't a place at all—it's a release from the straitjacket of delusion. If you demand that a physical place be specified, then it can be where you are sitting right now. For Siddhartha it was on top of a flat stone and some dried kusha grass under a bodhi tree in the Indian state of Bihar. Anyone can visit that physical location even today. Siddhartha's version of freedom is nonexclusive. It is attainable in this life, depending on the courage, wisdom, and diligence of the individual. There is no one who doesn't have this potential, including beings caught in the hell realms.

It was not Siddhartha's aim to be happy. His path does not ultimately lead to happiness. Instead it is a direct route to freedom from suffering, freedom from delusion and confusion. Thus nirvana is neither happiness nor unhappiness—it goes beyond all such dualistic concepts. Nirvana is peace. Siddhartha's aim in teaching the dharma is to completely free people like Jack, who suffers from fear of snakes. This means that Jack must go beyond the relief of realizing that he is in no danger from a snake. He must realize that there was never a snake to begin with, only a Giorgio Armani tie. In other words, Siddhartha's aim is to relieve Jack's suffering and then to help him realize that there was no inherently existing cause of suffering in the first place.

We could say that simply understanding the truth brings about the attainment of enlightenment. To the extent that we understand the truth, we can progress through the stages of enlightenment, called "bodhisattva levels." If a child is frightened by a hideous monster at the theater, the fear can be alleviated by introducing the child to the actor out of costume backstage. Similarly, to the degree that you can see behind all phenomena and understand the truth, you are liberated. Even if the actor only takes off his mask, the fear is lessened. Likewise, if one partially understands the truth, there is an equivalent liberation.

A sculptor may create a beautiful woman out of marble, but he should know better than to have passion toward his creation. Like Pygmalion with his statue of Galatea, we create our friends and our enemies as well, but we forget that it is so. Because of our lack of mindfulness, our creations are transformed into something solid and real, and we become ever more entangled. When you fully realize, not just intellectually, that everything is just your creation, you will be free.

Even though happiness is considered a mere concept, Buddhist texts still use terms like *great bliss* to describe enlightenment. Nirvana can indeed be understood as a joyful state, because having no confusion and no ignorance, no happiness and no unhappiness, is bliss. Seeing the source of confusion and ignorance, the snake for example, as never having existed, is even better. You feel great relief when you awaken from a nightmare, but bliss would be to never have dreamed in the first place. In this sense, bliss is not the same as happiness. Siddhartha emphasized to his followers the futility of seeking peace and happiness, in this world or in the afterlife, if they were serious about freeing themselves from samsara.

THE TRAP OF HAPPINESS

Buddha had a cousin named Nanda who was deeply, passionately in love with one of his wives. They were obsessed with each other, inseparable day or night. Buddha knew it was time for his cousin to wake up from this indulgence, so he went to Nanda's palace to beg for alms. Visitors were customarily turned away because Nanda was busy with lovemaking, but Buddha had special influence. For many lifetimes he had never told a lie, and because of this merit he had earned the power of persuasive speech. When the guard delivered the message that Buddha was at the door, Nanda reluctantly got up from his love nest. He felt obligated to at least greet his cousin. Before he went out, his wife wet her thumb and traced a circle of saliva on his forehead, telling him that he must come back to her before it dried. But when Nanda went to offer alms, Buddha invited him to see something truly rare and fantastic. Nanda tried to find an excuse not to join the sightseeing tour, but Buddha insisted.

The two journeyed to a mountain where many langurs dwelled, including one particularly gnarly one-eyed she-monkey. Buddha asked Nanda, "Who is more beautiful, your wife or this monkey?" Of course, Nanda replied that his wife was the most beautiful, and he described all her delights. Speaking of her made him realize that the spit on his forehead had long-ago dried up, and he longed to return to his home. But instead Buddha dragged Nanda to Tushita Heaven, where hundreds of beautiful goddesses and mountains of heavenly wealth were on display. Buddha asked, "Who is more beautiful, your wife or these goddesses?" This time Nanda bowed and replied that his wife was like a she-monkey compared to these goddesses. Buddha then showed Nanda an opulent throne that stood vacant amid all the treasures, goddesses, and guards. Awestruck, Nanda asked, "Who sits here?" Buddha told him to ask the goddesses. They said, "On Earth there is a man named Nanda who is soon going to become a monk. Because of his virtuous actions he will be reborn in heaven and assume this throne so that we can serve him." Immediately Nanda asked Buddha to ordain him.

They returned to the mundane world and Nanda became a monk. Buddha then summoned a second cousin, Ananda, and told him to make sure that all the other monks shunned Nanda. They were to avoid him at all costs. "Do not mingle, because you have different intentions, therefore your views are different and your actions will of course be different," said Buddha. "You are looking for enlightenment, and he is looking for happiness." The monks avoided Nanda, who became sad and lonely. He spoke to Buddha about feeling left out. Buddha told Nanda to come with him again. This time they journeyed to a hell realm, where they witnessed all kinds of torture, dismemberment, and asphyxiation. In the center of all the activity stood an enormous cauldron, with all the hell staff gathered around making grand preparations. Buddha told Nanda to ask what they were doing. "Oh," they replied, "on Earth there is a man named Nanda who is a monk now. Because of that he will go to heaven for a long time. But because he hasn't cut the root of samsara, he will be too caught up with the enjoyments of the god realm and won't seek to generate more good circumstances. His merit will become exhausted and he will fall straight into this cauldron so we can boil him."

At that moment Nanda realized that he must renounce not only unhappiness but happiness as well.

Nanda's story illustrates how we all get caught up in pleasurable indulgences. Like Nanda, we are quick to forsake one happiness when a better happiness is presented. The one-eyed monkey reinforced Nanda's perception of his wife's supreme beauty, but he didn't hesitate to give her up when he saw the goddesses. If enlightenment were merely happiness, then it too could be discarded when something better comes along. Happiness is a flimsy premise upon which to base one's life.

We human beings tend to think of enlightened beings within our own context. It's easier to imagine a hypothetical enlightened being off in the hazy distance, rather than a present, living, breathing enlightened being, because in our mind such a being must be spectacular, possessing superior traits and talents in addition to all the best human characteristics. Some of us may think that we can gain enlightenment by trying really hard. But with such an exalted image in our minds, "trying hard" probably means exerting ourselves and sacrificing all kinds of goodies for millions of lifetimes. These thoughts may arise when we bother to think about it, but most of the time we can't be bothered. It's too tiring. When we see how difficult it is to get rid of our mundane habits, enlightenment seems out of reach. If I can't even stop smoking, how can I think about stopping the habits of passion, anger, and denial? Many of us think that we must appoint someone like a savior or a guru to do the cleansing for us because we don't have confidence to do it alone. But all this pessimism isn't necessary if we have the right information about the truth of interdependence and a little bit of discipline to apply it.

HOPE AND PRIMORDIAL PURITY

Enlightenment transcends doubt, just as knowledge gained through experience transcends doubt. We must come to a complete understanding that the defilements and confusions that obstruct our enlightenment are not fixed in place. As stubborn and permanent-seeming as our obstacles may be, they are actually unstable compounded phenomena. Understanding the logic that compounded phenomena are dependent and can be manipulated leads us to see their impermanent nature and to reach the conclusion that they can be completely removed.

Our true nature is like a wineglass, and our defilements and obscurations are like dirt and fingerprints. When we buy the glass, it has no inherently existing fingerprints. When it becomes soiled, the habitual mind thinks the glass *is* dirty, not that the glass *has* dirt. Its nature is not dirty, it's a glass with some dirt and fingerprints on it. These impurities can be removed. If the glass *is* dirty, then the only option is to get rid of the glass itself, because the dirt and the glass would be united into one thing: a dirty glass. But that is not the case. The dirt, fingerprints, and other substances appeared on the glass due to a number of circumstances. They are temporary. We can use all kinds of different methods to wash the dirt away. We can wash the glass in the river or the sink or the dishwasher, or we can ask the maid to clean it. But no matter what method we use, the intent is to remove the dirt, not the glass. There is a big distinction between washing the glass and washing the dirt. We might contend that it's just a semantic distinction, that when we say we are washing the dishes, we mean we are washing the impurities off of the dishes, and in that case Siddhartha would agree. But if we think that the glass is somehow different than it was before, there is a misconception. Because the glass has no inherent fingerprints, when you remove the dirt, the glass isn't transformed—it's the same glass you bought at the store.

When we think of ourselves as inherently angry and ignorant, and we doubt our ability to achieve enlightenment, we are thinking that our true nature is permanently impure and defiled. But like the fingerprints on the wineglass, these emotions are not part of our true nature; we have only gathered pollutants from all sorts of unfavorable situations, such as associating with nonvirtuous people or not understanding the consequences of our actions. The primordial absence of defilements, the pure nature of the self, is often called "buddhanature." Yet the defilements and the resulting emotions have been there for so long and have become so strong that they are our second nature, always shadowing us. It is not surprising that we think there is no hope.

To regain hope, those on the Buddhist path may start out thinking, *My wineglass can be cleaned,* or *My being can be purified of negativity.* This is the same slightly naive way of looking at the situation as Jack thinking the snake must be removed. Nevertheless, sometimes it is a necessary preparatory step before we can see the primordial true nature of things. If it is not possible to perceive the preexisting purity of all phenomena, at least believing that a pure state can be attained helps drive us forward. Like Jack wanting to get rid of the snake, we want to rid ourselves of obscurations, and we have the courage to try because we know it is possible. We must simply apply remedies to weaken the causes and conditions of our defilements or strengthen their opposition—for example, by generating love and compassion to conquer anger. Just as our enthusiasm for doing the dishes comes from trusting we can have a clean glass, our enthusiasm for eliminating our obscurations comes from trusting we have buddhanature. We have the confidence to put our dirty dishes in the dishwasher because we know that the food is removable. If we were asked to wash charcoal to make it white, we would not have such enthusiasm and confidence.

FLASHING THROUGH THE STORMY DARKNESS

But how does one detect buddhanature in the midst of so much ignorance, darkness, and confusion? The first sign of hope for sailors lost at sea is to catch sight of a beam of light flashing through the stormy darkness. Navigating toward it, they come to the source of the light, the lighthouse. Love and compassion are like the light emanating from buddhanature. Initially buddhanature is a mere concept beyond our view, but if we generate love and compassion, we can eventually move toward it. It may be difficult to see the buddhanature in those who are lost in the darkness of greed, hate, and ignorance. Their buddhanature is so distant, we might think it is nonexistent. But even within the darkest and most violent people, there are flashes of love and compassion, however brief and faint. If these rare glimpses are attended to, and if energy is invested to move in the direction of the light, their buddhanature can be uncovered.

For this reason, love and compassion are praised as the safest path to the total absence of ignorance. Siddhartha's first act of compassion took place during an early incarnation in an unlikely place—not as a bodhisattva but as a resident of a hell realm, where he found himself as the result of his own bad karma. He and a fellow hell being were forced to drag a chariot through the hell fires while a demon master rode in back, whipping them mercilessly. Siddhartha was still quite strong, but his companion was very weak and was being targeted even more viciously because of it.

The sight of his companion being whipped sent a pang of compassion through Siddhartha. He begged the demon, "Please let him go, let me carry the burden for both of us." Enraged, the demon bashed Siddhartha's head in and Siddhartha died, to be reincarnated in a higher realm. That spark of compassion at the point of death continued to grow and become brighter in his later reincarnations.

Along with love and compassion, there are myriad paths available to bring us closer to realizing buddhanature. Even if we only intellectually understand the basic goodness of ourselves and all beings, this understanding brings us closer to accomplishment. It is as if we have misplaced a precious diamond ring, but at least we know it is inside our treasure chest, not lost on some vast mountainside.

Although we use words such as *achieving, wishing,* and *praying* for enlightenment, ultimately we don't acquire enlightenment from an external source. A more correct way to put it is *discovering* the enlightenment that has always been there. Enlightenment is part of our true nature. Our true nature is like a golden statue; however, it is still in its mold, which is like our defilements and ignorance. Because ignorance and emotion are not an inherent part of our nature, just as the mold is not part of the statue, there is such a thing as primordial purity. When the mold is broken, the statue emerges. When our defilements are removed, our true buddhanature is revealed. But it is important to understand that buddhanature is not a divine, truly existing soul or essence.

HOW DOES IT FEEL?

We might still wonder, *What is this enlightenment if it is not happiness or unhappiness?* How does an enlightened being appear and function? How does it feel to discover our buddhanature?

In Buddhist texts, when these questions are posed, the answer is usually that it's beyond our conception, inexpressible. Many seem to have misunderstood this as a sly way of not answering the question. But actually that *is* the answer. Our logic, language, and symbols are so limited, we cannot even fully express something so mundane as the sense of relief; words are inadequate to fully transmit the total experience of relief to another person. If even quantum physicists find it difficult to find words to express their theories, then how can we expect to find a vocabulary for enlightenment? While we are caught in our current state, where only a limited amount of logic and language is used and where emotions still grip us, we can only imagine what it is like to be enlightened. But sometimes, with diligence and inferential logic, we can get a good approximation, just as when you see smoke coming from a mountain peak, you can make a calculated guess that there is a fire. Using what we have, we can begin to see and accept that obscurations are due to causes and conditions that can be manipulated and ultimately cleansed. Imagining the absence of our defiled emotions and negativity is the first step to understanding the nature of enlightenment.

Suppose you are suffering from a headache. Your immediate wish is for relief, which is possible because you recognize that the headache is not part of your innate being. Next you try to determine what caused the headache—lack of sleep, for example. Then you apply the proper remedy to remove the headache, such as taking aspirin or lying down for a nap.

In his first sermon, at Varanasi, Siddhartha taught the following four steps, known popularly as the four noble truths: know the suffering; abandon the causes of suffering; apply the path to the cessation of suffering; know that suffering can end. Some might wonder why Siddhartha needed to point out, "Know the suffering." Aren't we intelligent enough to know when we are in pain? Unfortunately only when pain is in its most fully blossomed state do we recognize it as pain and suffering. It is difficult to convince someone who is blissfully licking an ice cream cone that he is suffering. But then he remembers his doctor's warning to lower his cholesterol and lose weight. And if you explore this seeming pleasure closely from the time he started craving ice cream all the way to his worry about fat and cholesterol, you'll see that it has been an anxious time.

It's easy to accept that emotions such as anger can be controlled with the proper remedy perhaps for one afternoon, but it is mentally challenging to accept that an emotion can disappear forever. If we can imagine someone who has partially removed anger, generally appearing calm and tranquil, we can take it a step further and imagine a person who has permanently removed anger. But how does someone who has gone beyond all emotions behave? The blindly devoted might imagine some docile being, perhaps sitting cross-legged on a cloud. The skeptics, however, may think that this person must function like a vegetable, unresponsive and dull . . . if he even exists at all.

Even though the enlightened state is inexpressible, and enlightened beings cannot be identified by the ordinary mind, we can still ask, "Who was Siddhartha? What did he do that was so amazing and so powerful? What extraordinary feats did he perform?" In Buddhism, an enlightened being is not judged by supernatural acts such as flying, or by physical attributes such as a third eye. Even though Buddha is frequently described as looking very serene, golden in color, with gentle hands and a regal manner, these descriptions appeal primarily to naive peasants and Jack-like beings. In the strict Buddhist scriptures, Buddha's abilities to fly and to perform magic are not flaunted. In fact, time and again in the pith instructions, Buddha's followers are warned not to be impressed by these inconsequential traits. Although he may have possessed such talents, they were never considered his greatest achievements. His greatest achievement was understanding the truth, because it is the understanding of the truth that frees us from suffering once and for all. That is the true miracle. Buddha saw the same old age and sickness and death that we see, but he was driven to find the root causes; and that, too, is a miracle. His realization that all compounded things are impermanent was his ultimate triumph. Instead of flaunting victory over some externally existing enemy, he found that the real enemy is our clinging to the self; and defeating that self-clinging is a miracle far greater than all supernatural miracles, real or imagined.

Although modern scientists take credit for discovering that time and space are relative, Siddhartha came to the same conclusion 2,500 years ago, without any research grants or scientific laboratories—and that, too, is a miracle. Unlike many of his contemporaries (and like many of us today) who were stuck with the notion that our freedom depends on the grace of others, he discovered that every being is by nature pure. Equipped with this knowledge, all beings have the power to free themselves. Instead of retreating into a lifetime of contemplation, Buddha had the incredible compassion to share his breakthrough discoveries with all beings, no matter how difficult to teach and to understand. He designed a path with tens of thousands of methods, from simple ones like offering incense, sitting straight, and watching the breath to complex visualizations and meditations. This was his extraordinary power.

THE ADVANTAGES OF GOING BEYOND SPACE AND TIME

When Siddhartha became enlightened, he became known as the Buddha. *Buddha* isn't a person's name, it is the label for a state of mind. The word *buddha* is defined as one quality with two aspects: "accomplished one" and "awakened one." In other words, one who has purified defilements and one who has attained knowledge. Through his realization under the bodhi tree, Buddha awoke from the dualistic state that is mired in concepts such as subject and object. He realized that nothing compounded can permanently exist. He realized that no emotion leads one to bliss if it stems from clinging to ego. He realized that there is no truly existing self and no truly existing phenomena to be perceived. And he realized that even enlightenment is beyond concepts. These realizations are what we call "Buddha's wisdom," an awareness of the whole truth. Buddha is referred to as omniscient. That doesn't mean that Buddha went to every university in the world and memorized every book. Such study does not equate to awakened knowledge, for it is a dualistic knowledge, which is based on objects and subjects and bound by its own limitations, rules, and goals. As we can clearly see, with all the scientific knowledge we have today, the world hasn't improved; in fact, it may even be worse. To be omniscient doesn't mean to be learned. Thus to speak of someone who knows everything means someone who has no "not knowing" and no ignorance.

Buddha went a step further and pointed out the truth of the awakened mind to others so that they, too, could break the cycle of suffering, and for this compassion he is most revered. If someone is unknowingly about to walk through a field of land mines, we might be able to quickly defuse the mines without letting him know. But that only protects the person temporarily, and it doesn't provide the complete truth. To explain to him that there are land mines in that direction for several miles saves him from both immediate and future suffering. It allows him to go forward and even share the knowledge with others. In the same way, Buddha taught people to be generous if they wish to be rich and to be compassionate if they wish to conquer their enemies. But he also advised that if they want to be rich, first be content; and if they want to conquer the enemy, first conquer their own anger. Ultimately he taught that suffering can be cut at the root by dismantling the self, for if there is no self, there is no sufferer.

In appreciation for his teachings, Siddhartha's followers venerated him with songs and prayers in which he is praised for being so powerful that he could put the entire universe on top of one atom. With similar reverence, some followers wish to be reborn in the realm called "the buddhafield." The buddhafield is described as a pure land the size of one infinitesimal particle, upon which the same number of buddhas as there are atoms in the universe teach their own disciples. As with Milarepa's yak horn, a nonbeliever can read this as a religious fairy tale, whereas a believer might uncritically accept the description, thinking, *Of course Buddha can do this—he is omnipotent.* But if we can think of the truth in terms of emptiness, realizing that there is no such thing as smallest and biggest or any other dualistic distinctions, then it is clear that Buddha did not need muscle and brawn to pick up the world and place it on an atom. The very understanding that there is no big or small was all the force necessary. It is possible to remove the habit that prevents us from seeing in this way, but our limited logic gets in the way. We are like an anorexic or bulimic who, even though she may be beautiful and slender, simply cannot accept what she sees in the mirror, even while others can't see why she thinks she is fat.

Buddha removed all such obfuscations and saw everything—time, space, gender, values—to be absent of dualism, so the universe could rest on a single atom. For this realization, his poetic devotees praised him for going "beyond space and time." Even Siddhartha's closest disciples, the arhats, are renowned for seeing the sky and the palm of a hand as the same size, a piece of dirt and a piece of gold as having equal value.

When Siddhartha reached enlightenment, he didn't make time stop or reach to the end of time. He simply was no longer stained by the concept of time. When we say Siddhartha removed all obscurations of time and space, it is not that he broke the time machine or physically dismantled a compass—he went completely beyond all concepts of time and space.

Although the actual experience of going beyond time and space is unfathomable to us time-slaves, it is possible to get a sense of the elasticity of these concepts within our mundane existence. Even a romantic crush can stretch and bend time. We meet someone, we daydream about becoming soul mates, getting married, having children and even grandchildren. But then something like a bit of saliva dripping out of the loved one's mouth snaps us back to reality, and all those future generations vanish.

Because the advantages of going beyond space and time are so incomprehensible, we are not drawn to understand them. We are too accustomed to the world that depends on time and space to exert ourselves for such intangible rewards. It may be easier to grasp the aspect of enlightenment that is beyond emotional distinctions of good and bad, pleasure and pain, praise and criticism, and other dualistic emotions. Our reliance on space and time is understandable—they are very useful for now—but these other distinctions are useless to the point of absurdity. Dualism has us so entangled that we spend millions of dollars every year to keep up appearances. If we were wandering alone in the desert, there would be no point in looking fabulous, so obviously we want to make ourselves look good in relation to others, to attract them, to compete with them, to be accepted by them. When someone says, "Oh, you have nice legs," we are thrilled and continue preening and fishing for compliments. These compliments are like honey on a sharp knife.

Many of us are so engrossed with our own concepts of beauty that we don't perceive that our version of what is attractive may actually repel others. We fall victim to our own concepts and to our vanity. This vanity feeds the cosmetic industry, which is one of the causes and conditions that literally destroys the environment. When we receive a good amount of praise peppered with a little criticism, all of our attention goes to the criticism. Compliments are taken for granted because of our insatiable appetite for praise. One who desires unending praise and attention is like a butterfly trying to find the edge of the sky.

NO DISTINCTIONS, NO CONCEPTS, NO LEASH

Along with conventional concepts of time and space, Buddha dropped all subtle emotional dualistic distinctions. He had no preference for praise over criticism, gain over loss, happiness over unhappiness, fame over obscurity. He was not swayed by optimism or pessimism. One did not have a stronger attraction or warrant a greater investment of energy than the other. Imagine no longer falling prey to small praises and criticisms, hearing them as Buddha did—as mere sounds, like an echo. Or hearing them as we would on our deathbed. We might take some pleasure in listening to our loved ones praise how beautiful and wonderful we are, but at the same time we would be detached and unaffected. We would no longer cling to the words. Imagine being above bribes and other persuasions because all worldly temptations seem uninteresting, like a salad to a tiger. If we couldn't be bought by praise or defeated by criticism, we would have incredible strength. We would be extraordinarily free, there would be no more unnecessary hopes and fears, sweat and blood, and emotional reactions. We would finally be able to practice "I don't give a damn." Free from chasing after and avoiding other people's acceptance and rejection, we would be able to appreciate what we have in the present moment. Most of the time we are trying to make the good things last, or we are thinking about replacing them with something even better in the future, or we are sunk in the past, reminiscing about happier times. Ironically, we never truly appreciated the experience for which we are nostalgic because we were too busy clinging to our hopes and fears at the time.

Where we are like children at the beach, busy building sand castles, sublime beings are like adults watching from under an umbrella. The children are carried away with their creations, fighting over shells and shovels, terrified of the waves coming closer. They go through all kinds of emotions. But the adults lie nearby, sipping a coconut cocktail, watching, not judging, not feeling pride when a sand castle is built very nicely and not feeling anger or sadness when someone accidentally steps on the turret. They are not caught up in the drama the way the children are. What more enlightenment could one ask for?

The closest simile to enlightenment in the secular world is "freedom"; in fact the concept of freedom is a driving force in our personal lives and our societies. We dream of a time and place where we can do whatever we like—the American Dream. In our speeches and our constitutions we chant "freedom" and "the rights of the individual" like mantras, yet deep down we don't really want them. If we were granted total freedom, we probably wouldn't know what to do with it. We don't have the courage or the ability to take advantage of true freedom because we are not free from our own pride, greed, hope, and fear. If everyone were to suddenly vanish from the earth except for one person, we can imagine total freedom for that person—he could shout and walk around naked, break the law—even though there would be no law, and no witness. But sooner or later he is going to get bored and lonely and wish for companions. The very idea of relationship requires giving up some of our freedom to the other. So if the lone man's wish comes true and he is granted one companion, it's likely the companion will do as he or she pleases and may very well compromise his freedom, intentionally or unintentionally. Who is to blame? The lone man, for it was his own boredom that invited his downfall. Without boredom and loneliness, he could still be free.

We do a good job of limiting our own freedoms. Even if we could, we would not walk around in our birthday suit or wear a dead fish as a tie at a job interview, because we want to impress people and win friends. We may not explore alternative or ethnic cultures, however much wisdom they offer, because we don't want to be branded as hippies.

We live behind bars of responsibility and conformity. We make a big issue of individual rights, privacy, the right to bear arms, and free speech, but we don't want to live next door to a terrorist. When it comes to others, we want to impose a few rules. If others are totally free, you may not get everything you want. Their freedom could limit your freedom. When trains are blown up in Madrid and buildings in New York are reduced to rubble, we blame the CIA for letting terrorists roam freely. We think it's the government's job to protect us from bullies. But the bullies and terrorists see themselves as freedom fighters. Meanwhile, we want to be politically correct and holders of justice, so if our ethnic-looking neighbor is nabbed by the federal agents, we may protest. It is especially easy to be politically correct about issues that are far removed from us. Either way, there is a risk of becoming the victims of our own political correctness.

RENUNCIATION: THE SKY IS THE LIMIT

If we are serious about achieving enlightenment, we need the strength to renounce the things that are a big deal for us, and we need a great deal of courage to step onto the path alone. Those who do not pursue praise and gain, those who do not shun criticism and loss, may be stigmatized as abnormal or even insane. When observed from an ordinary point of view, enlightened beings may seem insane because they don't negotiate, they cannot be lured or swayed by material gain, they don't get bored, they don't look for thrills, they have no face to lose, they do not conform to rules of etiquette, they never employ hypocrisy for personal gain, they never do things to impress people, and they don't display their talents and powers just for the sake of it. But if it benefits others, these saints will do anything necessary, from having perfect table manners to leading a Fortune 500 company. In 2,500 years of Buddhist history there have probably been countless enlightened beings who were never identified or who were banished for being insane. Very few were appreciated for possessing what we call "crazy wisdom." But when we think about it, we are the ones who are really insane, falling head over heels for echolike praise, brooding over criticism, and grasping at happiness.

Forget about going beyond time and space; even going beyond praise and criticism seems out of reach. But when we begin to understand, not only intellectually but emotionally, that all compounded things are impermanent, then our grasping lessens. Our conviction that our thoughts and possessions are valuable, important, and permanent begins to soften. If we were to be informed that we have only two days left to live, our actions would change. We would not be preoccupied with putting our shoes in line, ironing our underwear, or stockpiling expensive perfumes. We might still go shopping, but with a new attitude. If we know, even a little bit, that some of our familiar concepts, feelings, and objects exist only as a dream, we develop a much better sense of humor. Recognizing the humor in our situation prevents suffering. We still experience emotions, but they can no longer play tricks on us or pull the wool over our eyes. We can still fall in love, but without fear of being rejected. We will use our best perfume and face cream instead of saving them for a special occasion. Thus every day becomes a special day.

Buddha's qualities are inexpressible. They are just like the sky, which has no end in space. Our language and our analytical powers can only go as far as the concept of the universe. At some point a bird that flies higher and higher to find the end of the sky will reach its limit and have to return to earth.

The best metaphor for our experience in this world is an epic dream that has a number of complex, intertwining stories, ups and downs, dramas and thrills. If an episode of the dream is fraught with devils and beasts, we hope to escape. When we open our eyes to see the fan turning on the ceiling, we are relieved. For the sake of communication, we say, "I dreamed the devil was chasing me," and we feel relief at having escaped the clutches of the devil. But it is not as if the devil has gone away. The devil never entered your room during the night, and while you were having that hideous experience with him, he also was not there. When you are awake into enlightenment, you have never been a sentient being, you have never struggled. From then on, you do not have to be on guard against the devil's return. When you become enlightened, you cannot think back to when you were an ignorant being. No more meditation is needed. There is nothing to remember, because you have never forgotten anything.

As Buddha said in the *Prajnaparamita Sutra,* all phenomena are like a dream and an illusion, even enlightenment is like a dream and an illusion. And if there is anything greater or grander than enlightenment, that, too, is like a dream and an illusion. His disciple, the great Nagarjuna, wrote that the Lord Buddha has not stated that after abandoning samsara there exists nirvana. The nonexistence of samsara is nirvana. A knife becomes sharp as the result of two exhaustions—the exhaustion of the whetstone and the exhaustion of the metal. In the same way, enlightenment is the result of the exhaustion of defilements and the exhaustion of the antidote of the defilements. Ultimately one must abandon the path to enlightenment. If you still define yourself as a Buddhist, you are not a buddha yet.

Conclusion

*T*hese days we often encounter people who mix and blend religions to suit their comfort level. Trying to be non-sectarian, they attempt to explain Christian concepts from Buddha's point of view, or to find similarities between Buddhism and Sufism, or between Zen and business. Of course, one can always find at least small similarities between any two things in existence—but I don't think such comparisons are necessary. Even though all religions begin with some kind of philanthropic aim, usually to relieve suffering, they have fundamental differences. They are all like medicines; and like medicines, they are designed to reduce suffering, but they vary depending on the patient and the ailment. If you have poison ivy, the proper treatment is calamine lotion. If you have leukemia, you don't try to find the similarities between calamine lotion and chemotherapy so that you can justify applying calamine lotion because it's more convenient. Similarly, there is no need to confuse religions.

In these pages I have attempted to provide a glimpse into the fundamentals of the Buddhist view. In all religions the view is the foundation of the practice, because the view determines our motivation and actions. It's so true that "appearances can be deceiving." We truly can't judge our next-door neighbors solely by the way they look. So obviously we can't judge something as personal as religion by superficial appearance. We can't even judge religions by the actions, ethics, morality, or codes of conduct they promote.

THE VIEW IS THE FINAL REFERENCE POINT

The *view* is the core of any religion. At an interfaith conference we may have no choice but to be diplomatic and agree that all religions are basically the same. But in fact they have very different views, and no one but you yourself can judge if one view is better than the other. Only you as an individual, with your own mental capacity, taste, feelings, and upbringing, can choose the view that works for you. Like an abundant buffet, the variety of approaches offers something for everyone. For example, the Jain message of *ahimsa* is so beautiful that one wonders why this great religion is not flourishing like other religions. And the Christian message of love and salvation has brought peace and harmony to the hearts of millions.

The outward appearance of these religions can seem foreign and illogical to outsiders. Many of us are understandably apprehensive about age-old religions and superstitions that lack apparent reason. For example, many people are puzzled by the maroon robes and shaved heads of Buddhist monks because they seem irrelevant to science, economy, and life in general. I can't help wondering what such people would think if they were transported to a Tibetan monastery and faced with paintings of wrathful deities and naked ladies in sexual positions. They might think that they were seeing some exotic aspects of *The Kama Sutra*, or even worse—evidence of depravity or demon worship.

Outsiders might also be appalled at seeing Jain practitioners walking naked or Hindus worshipping gods that resemble cows and monkeys. Some find it difficult to understand why Muslims use their profound philosophy of forbidding idol worship as justification for demolishing the sacred icons of other religions, while in Mecca, one of Islam's most sacred sites, the Ka'aba, *Hajr-e-Aswad* (the sacred black stone), is a physical object of worship and the destination of millions of Muslim pilgrims each year. For those who have no understanding of Christianity, it may be inconceivable why the Christians don't pick a story out of Christ's heyday rather than his most gloomy episode on the cross. They may find it incomprehensible that the central icon, the cross, makes the savior seem so helpless. But these are all appearances. Judging or valuing a path or religion by such appearances is not wise, and it can foster prejudice.

Strict conduct can't be used to define a religion either. Adherence to rules does not make a good person. It is believed that Hitler was a vegetarian and very careful about his grooming. But discipline and smart outfits are not in themselves holy. And who determines what is "good" in the first place? What is wholesome in one religion is unwholesome or inconsequential in another. For example, Sikh men never cut their hair and beards, whereas monks in both Eastern and Western traditions often shave their heads, and Protestants can do as they please with their hair. Each religion has profound explanations for their symbols and practices—why they don't eat pork or prawns, why they are required to shave or prohibited from shaving. But within these infinite dos and don'ts, each religion must have a fundamental view, and that view is what matters most.

The view is the final reference point to determine whether or not an action is justifiable. Action is valued by how well it complements one's view. For example, if you live in Venice Beach, California, and you have the view that it's good to be slim, your motivation is to lose weight, you meditate on the beach about how nice that would be, and your action might be to avoid carbohydrates. Now suppose you are a sumo wrestler in Tokyo. Your view is that it's good to be enormously fat, your motivation is to gain weight, and you meditate on how you can't be a skinny sumo wrestler. Your action is to eat as much rice and doughnuts as possible. The act of eating a doughnut is therefore good or bad, depending on your view. Thus we can mistakenly consider someone who abstains from meat to be a compassionate person, when actually their view is simply that meat is bad because it raises their cholesterol.

Ultimately no one can judge other people's actions without fully understanding their view.

All methods of Buddhism can be explained with the four seals—all compounded phenomena are impermanent, all emotions are pain, all things have no inherent existence, and enlightenment is beyond concepts. Every act and deed encouraged by Buddhist scriptures is based on these four truths, or seals.

In the Mahayana sutras, Buddha advised his followers not to eat meat. Not only is it nonvirtuous to bring direct harm to another being, but the act of eating meat does not complement the four seals. This is because when you eat meat, on some level you are doing it for survival—to sustain yourself. This desire to survive is connected to wanting to be permanent, to live longer at the expense of the life of another being. If putting an animal into your mouth would absolutely guarantee an extension of your life, then, from a selfish point of view, there would be reason to do so. But no matter how many dead bodies you stuff into your mouth, you are going to die one of these days. Maybe even sooner.

One may also consume meat for bourgeois reasons—savoring caviar because it is extravagant, eating tigers' penises for virility, consuming boiled bird's nests to maintain youthful-appearing skin. One cannot find a more selfish act than that—for your vanity a life is extinguished. In a reverse situation, we humans cannot even bear a mosquito bite, let alone imagine ourselves confined in crowded cages with our beaks cut off waiting to be slaughtered, along with our family and friends, or being fattened up in a pen to become human burgers.

The attitude that our vanity is worth another's life is clinging to the self. Clinging to the self is ignorance; and as we have seen, ignorance leads to pain. In the case of eating meat it also causes others to experience pain. For this reason, the Mahayana sutras describe the practice of putting oneself in the place of these creatures and refraining from eating meat out of a sense of compassion. When Buddha prohibited consumption of meat, he meant *all* meats. He didn't single out beef for sentimental reasons, or pork because it is dirty, nor did he say that it's OK to eat fish because they have no soul.

THE BEAUTIFUL LOGIC OF THE FOUR SEALS

As an example of the first seal—impermanence—consider generosity. When we begin to realize the first truth, we see everything as transitory and without value, as if it belonged in a Salvation Army donation bag. We don't necessarily have to give it all away, but we have no clinging to it. When we see that our possessions are all impermanent compounded phenomena, that we cannot cling to them forever, generosity is already practically accomplished.

Understanding the second seal, that all emotions are pain, we see that the miser, the self, is the main culprit, providing nothing but a feeling of poverty. Therefore, by not clinging to the self, we find no reason to cling to our possessions, and there is no more pain of miserliness. Generosity becomes an act of joy.

Realizing the third seal, that all things have no inherent existence, we see the futility of clinging because whatever we are clinging to has no truly existing nature. It's like dreaming that you are distributing a billion dollars to strangers on the street. You can give generously because it's dream money, and yet you are able to reap all the fun of the experience. Generosity based on these three views inevitably makes us realize that there is no goal. It is not a sacrifice endured in order to get recognition or to ensure a better rebirth.

Generosity without a price tag, expectations, or strings provides a glimpse into the fourth view, the truth that liberation, enlightenment, is beyond conception.

If we measure the perfection of a virtuous action, such as generosity, by material standards—how much poverty is eliminated—we can never reach perfection. Destitution and the desires of the destitute are endless. Even the desires of the wealthy are endless; in fact the desires of humans can never be fully satisfied. But according to Siddhartha, generosity should be measured by the level of attachment one has to what is being given and to the self that is giving it. Once you have realized that the self and all its possessions are impermanent and have no truly existing nature, you have nonattachment, and that is perfect generosity. For this reason the first action encouraged in the Buddhist sutras is the practice of generosity.

A DEEPER UNDERSTANDING OF KARMA, PURITY, AND NONVIOLENCE

The concept of karma, the undeniable trademark of Buddhism, also falls within these four truths. When causes and conditions come together and there are no obstacles, consequences arise. Consequence *is* karma. This karma is gathered by consciousness—the mind, or the self. If this self acts out of greed or aggression, negative karma is generated. If a thought or action is motivated by love, tolerance, and a wish for others to be happy, positive karma is generated. Yet motivation, action, and the resulting karma are inherently like a dream, an illusion. Transcending karma, both good and bad, is nirvana. Any so-called good action that is *not* based on these four views is merely righteousness; it is not ultimately Siddhartha's path. Even if you were to feed all the hungry beings in the world, if you acted in complete absence of these four views, then it would be merely a good deed, not the path to enlightenment. In fact it might be a righteous act designed to feed and support the ego.

It is because of these four truths that Buddhists can practice purification. If one thinks that one is stained by negative karma or is weak or "sinful," and is frustrated, thinking that these obstacles are always getting in the way of realization, then one can take comfort in knowing that they are compounded and therefore impermanent and thus purifiable. On the other hand, if one feels lacking in ability or merit, one can take comfort knowing that merit can be accumulated through performing good deeds, because the lack of merit is impermanent and therefore changeable.

The Buddhist practice of nonviolence is not merely submissiveness with a smile or meek thoughtfulness. The fundamental cause of violence is when one is fixated on an extreme idea, such as justice or morality. This fixation usually stems from a habit of buying into dualistic views, such as bad and good, ugly and beautiful, moral and immoral. One's inflexible self-righteousness takes up all the space that would allow empathy for others. Sanity is lost. Understanding that all these views or values are compounded and impermanent, as is the person who holds them, violence is averted. When you have no ego, no clinging to the self, there is never a reason to be violent. When one understands that one's enemies are held under a powerful influence of their own ignorance and aggression, that they are trapped by their habits, it is easier to forgive them for their irritating behavior and actions. Similarly, if someone from the insane asylum insults you, there is no point in getting angry. When we transcend believing in the extremes of dualistic phenomena, we have transcended the causes of violence.

THE FOUR SEALS: A PACKAGE DEAL

In Buddhism, any action that establishes or enhances the four views is a rightful path. Even seemingly ritualistic practices, such as lighting incense or practicing esoteric meditations and mantras, are designed to help focus our attention on one or all of the truths.

Anything that contradicts the four views, including some action that may seem loving and compassionate, is not part of the path. Even emptiness meditation becomes pure negation, nothing but a nihilistic path, if it is not in compliance with the four truths.

For the sake of communication we can say that these four views are the spine of Buddhism. We call them "truths" because they are simply facts. They are not manufactured; they are not a mystical revelation of the Buddha. They did not become valid only after the Buddha began to teach. Living by these principles is not a ritual or a technique. They don't qualify as morals or ethics, and they can't be trademarked or owned. There is no such thing as an "infidel" or a "blasphemer" in Buddhism because there is no one to be faithful to, to insult, or to doubt. However, those who are not aware of or do not believe in these four facts are considered by Buddhists to be ignorant. Such ignorance is not cause for moral judgment. If someone doesn't believe that humans have landed on the moon, or thinks that the world is flat, a scientist wouldn't call him a blasphemer, just ignorant. Likewise, if he doesn't believe in these four seals, he is not an infidel. In fact, if someone were to produce proof that the logic of the four seals is faulty, that clinging to the self is actually not pain, or that some element defies impermanence, then Buddhists should willingly follow that path instead. Because what we seek is enlightenment, and enlightenment means realization of the truth. So far, though, in all these centuries no proof has arisen to invalidate the four seals.

If you ignore the four seals but insist on considering yourself a Buddhist merely out of a love affair with the traditions, then that is superficial devotion. The Buddhist masters believe that however you choose to label yourself, unless you have faith in these truths, you will continue to live in an illusory world, believing it to be solid and real. Although such belief temporarily provides the bliss of ignorance, ultimately it always leads to some form of anxiety. You then spend all your time solving problems and trying to get rid of the anxiety. Your constant need to solve problems becomes like an addiction. How many problems have you solved only to watch others arise? If you are happy with this cycle, then you have no reason to complain. But when you see that you will never come to the end of problem solving, that is the beginning of the search for inner truth. While Buddhism is not the answer to all the world's temporal problems and social injustices, if you happen to be searching and if you happen to have chemistry with Siddhartha, then you may find these truths agreeable. If that is the case, you should consider following him seriously.

RICHNESS WITHIN RENUNCIATION

As a follower of Siddhartha, you don't necessarily have to emulate his every action—you don't have to sneak out while your wife is sleeping. Many people think that Buddhism is synonymous with renunciation, leaving home, family, and job behind, and following the path of an ascetic. This image of austerity is partly due to the fact that a great number of Buddhists revere the mendicants in the Buddhist texts and teachings, just as the Christians admire Saint Francis of Assisi. We can't help being struck by the image of the

Buddha walking barefoot in Magadha with his begging bowl, or Milarepa in his cave subsisting on nettle soup. The serenity of a simple Burmese monk accepting alms captivates our imagination.

But there is also an entirely different variety of follower of the Buddha: King Ashoka, for example, who dismounted from his royal chariot, adorned with pearls and gold, and proclaimed his wish to spread the buddhadharma throughout the world. He knelt down, seized a fistful of sand, and proclaimed that he would build as many stupas as there were grains of sand in his hand. And in fact he kept his promise. So one can be a king, a merchant, a prostitute, a junkie, a chief executive officer, and still accept the four seals. Fundamentally it is not the act of leaving behind the material world that Buddhists cherish but the ability to see the habitual clinging to this world and ourselves and to renounce the clinging.

As we begin to understand the four views, we don't necessarily discard things; we begin instead to change our attitude toward them, thereby changing their value. Just because you have less than someone else doesn't mean that you are more morally pure or virtuous. In fact humility itself can be a form of hypocrisy. When we understand the essencelessness and impermanence of the material world, renunciation is no longer a form of self-flagellation. It doesn't mean that we're hard on ourselves. The word *sacrifice* takes on a different meaning. Equipped with this understanding, everything becomes about as significant as the saliva we spit on the ground. We don't feel sentimental about saliva. Losing such sentimentality is a path of bliss, *sugata*. When renunciation is understood as bliss, the stories of many other Indian princesses, princes, and warlords who once upon a time renounced their palace life become less outlandish.

This love of truth and veneration for the seekers of truth is an ancient tradition in countries like India. Even today, instead of looking down on renunciants, Indian society venerates them just as respectfully as we venerate professors at Harvard and Yale. Although the tradition is fading in this age when corporate culture reigns, you can still find naked, ash-clad sadhus who have given up successful law practices to become wandering mendicants. It gives me goose bumps to see how Indian society respects these people instead of shooing them away as disgraceful beggars or pests. I can't help but imagine them at the Marriott Hotel in Hong Kong. How would the nouveau-riche Chinese, desperately trying to copy Western ways, feel about these ash-clad sadhus? Would the doorman open the door for them? For that matter, how would the concierge at the Hotel Bel-Air in Los Angeles react? Instead of worshipping the truth and venerating sadhus, this is an age that worships billboards and venerates liposuction.

ADOPTING WISDOM, DROPPING DISTORTED MORALITIES

As you read this, you may be thinking, *I'm generous and I don't have that much attachment to my things.* It may be true that you aren't tightfisted, but in the midst of your generous activities, if someone walks off with your favorite pencil, you may get so angry that you want to bite his ear off. Or you may become completely disheartened if someone says, "Is that all you can give?" When we give, we are caught up in the notion of "generosity." We cling to the result—if not a good rebirth, at least recognition in this life, or maybe just a plaque on the wall. I have also met many people who think they are generous simply because they have given money to a certain museum, or even to their own children, from whom they expect a lifetime of allegiance.

If it is not accompanied by the four views, morality can be similarly distorted. Morality feeds the ego, leading us to become puritanical and to judge others whose morality is different from ours. Fixated on our version of morality, we look down on other people and try to impose our ethics on them, even if it means taking away their freedom. The great Indian scholar and saint Shantideva, himself a prince who renounced his kingdom, taught that it is impossible for us to avoid encountering anything and everything unwholesome, but if we can apply just one of these four views, we are protected from all nonvirtue. If you think the entire West is somehow satanic or immoral, it will be impossible to conquer and rehabilitate it, but if you have tolerance within yourself, this is equal to conquering. You can't smooth out the entire earth to make it easier to walk on with your bare feet, but by wearing shoes you protect yourself from rough, unpleasant surfaces.

If we can understand the four views not only intellectually but also experientially, we begin to free ourselves from fixating on things that are illusory. This freedom is what we call wisdom. Buddhists venerate wisdom above all else. Wisdom surpasses morality, love, common sense, tolerance, and vegetarianism. It is not a divine spirit that we seek from somewhere outside of ourselves. We invoke it by first hearing the teachings on the four seals—not accepting them at face value, but rather analyzing and contemplating them. If you are convinced that this path will clear some of your confusion and bring some relief, then you can actually put wisdom into practice.

In one of the oldest Buddhist teaching methods, the master gives his disciples a bone and instructs them to contemplate its origin. Through this contemplation, the disciples eventually see the bone as the end result of birth, birth as the end result of karmic formation, karmic formation as the end result of craving, and so on. Thoroughly convinced by the logic of cause, condition, and effect, they begin to apply awareness to every situation and every moment. This is what we call meditation. People who can bring us this kind of information and understanding are venerated as masters because, even though they have profound realization and could happily live in the forest, they are willing to stick around to explain the view to those who are still in the dark. Because this information liberates us from all kinds of unnecessary hiccups, we have an automatic appreciation for the explainer. So we Buddhists pay homage to the teacher.

Once you have intellectually accepted the view, you can apply any method that deepens your understanding and realization. In other words, you can use whatever techniques or practices help you to transform your habit of thinking that things are solid into the habit of seeing them as compounded, interdependent, and impermanent. This is true Buddhist meditation and practice, not just sitting still as if you were a paperweight.

Even though we know intellectually that we are going to die, this knowledge can be eclipsed by something as small as a casual compliment. Someone comments on how graceful our knuckles look, and the next thing we know we are trying to find ways to preserve these knuckles. Suddenly we feel that we have something to lose. These days we are constantly bombarded by so many new things to lose and so many things to gain. More than ever we need methods that remind us and help us get accustomed to the view, maybe even hanging a human bone from the rearview mirror, if not shaving your head and retreating to a cave. Combined with these methods, ethics and morality become useful. Ethics and morality may be secondary in Buddhism, but they are important when they bring us closer to the truth. But even if some action appears wholesome and positive, if it takes us away from the four truths, Siddhartha himself cautioned us to leave it be.

THE TEA AND THE TEACUP: WISDOM WITHIN CULTURE

The four seals are like tea, while all other means to actualize these truths—practices, rituals, traditions, and cultural trappings—are like a cup. The skills and methods are observable and tangible, but the truth is not. The challenge is not to get carried away by the cup. People are more inclined to sit straight in a quiet place on a meditation cushion than to contemplate which will come first, tomorrow or the next life. Outward practices are perceivable, so the mind is quick to label them as Buddhism; whereas the concept "all compounded things are impermanent" is not tangible and is difficult to label. It is ironic that evidence of impermanence is all around us, yet is not obvious to us.

The essence of Buddhism is beyond culture, but it is practiced by many different cultures, which use their traditions as the cup that holds the teachings. If the elements of these cultural trappings help other beings without causing harm, and if they don't contradict the four truths, then Siddhartha would encourage such practices.

Throughout the centuries so many brands and styles of cups have been produced, but however good the intention behind them, and however well they may work, they become a hindrance if we forget the tea inside. Even though their purpose is to hold the truth, we tend to focus on the means rather than the outcome. So people walk around with empty cups, or they forget to drink their tea. We human beings can become enchanted, or at least distracted, by the ceremony and color of Buddhist cultural practices. Incense and candles are exotic and attractive; impermanence and selflessness are not. Siddhartha himself said that the best way to worship is by simply remembering the principle of impermanence, the suffering of emotions, that phenomena have no inherent existence, and that nirvana is beyond concepts.

On a superficial level, Buddhism can seem ritualistic and religious. Buddhist disciplines such as maroon robes, rituals and ritual objects, incense and flowers, even monasteries, have form —they can be observed and photographed. We forget that they are a means to an end. We forget that one does not become a follower of Buddha by performing rituals or adopting disciplines such as becoming vegetarian or wearing robes. But the human mind loves symbols and rituals so much that they are almost inevitable and indispensable. Tibetan sand mandalas and Japanese Zen gardens are beautiful; they can inspire us and even be a means to understanding the truth. But the truth itself is neither beautiful nor not beautiful.

Although we can probably do without things like red hats, yellow hats, and black hats, there are some rituals and disciplines that are universally advisable. One cannot definitively say that it is wrong to meditate while lying in a hammock and holding a drink garnished with a small umbrella, as long as you are contemplating the truth. But antidotes such as sitting up straight actually have great benefit. Correct posture is not only accessible and economical, it has the power to deprive your emotions of their usual quick reflex that engrosses you and sends you adrift. It gives you a little space to become sober. Other institutionalized rituals, such as group ceremonies and religious hierarchical structures, may have some benefit, but it is important to note that they have been the targets of sarcasm of past masters. I personally think that these rituals must be the reason why many people in the West categorize Buddhism as a cult even though there isn't even the smallest trace of cultishness in the four truths.

Now that Buddhism is flourishing in the West, I have heard of people altering Buddhist teachings to fit the modern way of thinking. If there is anything to be adapted, it would be the rituals and symbols, not the truth itself. Buddha himself said that his discipline and methods should be adapted appropriately to time and place. But the four truths don't need to be updated or modified; and it's impossible to do so anyway. You can change the cup, but the tea remains pure. After surviving 2,500 years and traveling 40,781,035 feet from the bodhi tree in central India to Times Square in New York City, the concept "all compounded things are impermanent" still applies. Impermanence is still impermanence in Times Square. You cannot bend these four rules; there are no social or cultural exceptions.

Unlike some religions, Buddhism is not a survival kit for living that dictates how many husbands a wife should have, or where to pay taxes, or how to punish thieves. In fact, strictly speaking, Buddhists don't even have a ritual for wedding ceremonies. The purpose of Siddhartha's teaching was not to tell people what they wanted to hear. He taught because of his strong impulse to release others from their misconceptions and endless misunderstandings of the truth. However, in order to effectively explain these truths, Siddhartha taught with different manners and means, according to the needs of his different audiences. These different ways of teaching have now been labeled as different "schools" of Buddhism. But the fundamental view for all schools is the same.

It is normal for religions to have a leader. Some, such as the Roman Catholic Church, have an elaborate hierarchy, led by an all-powerful figure, to make decisions and pass judgments. Contrary to popular belief, Buddhism does not have such a figure or institution. The Dalai Lama is a secular leader for the Tibetan community in exile and a spiritual master to many people all over the world, but not necessarily for all Buddhists. There is no one authority with the power to decide who is a true Buddhist and who is not for all the forms and schools of Buddhism that exist in Tibet, Japan, Laos, China, Korea, Cambodia, Thailand, Vietnam, and the West. No one can declare who is punishable and who is not. This lack of a central power may bring chaos, but it is also a blessing because every source of power in every human institution is corruptible.

Buddha himself said, "You are your own master." Of course, if a learned master makes the effort to present the truth to you, you are a fortunate being. In some cases, such masters should be revered even more than the Buddha because although thousands of buddhas may have come, for you this person is the one who brought the truth to your doorstep. Finding a spiritual guide is entirely in your own hands. You are free to analyze him or her. When you are convinced of the master's authenticity, accepting, enduring, and enjoying him or her is part of your practice.

Respect is often confused with religious zeal. Because of unavoidable outward appearances, and also because of the lack of skill of some Buddhists, outsiders may think that we are worshipping Buddha and the lineage masters as though they were gods.

In case you are wondering how to decide which path is the right path, just remember that any path that doesn't contradict the four truths should be a safe path. Ultimately it is not the high-ranking masters who guard Buddhism, but the four truths that are the guardians.

I cannot emphasize enough that understanding the truth is the most important aspect of Buddhism. For centuries, scholars and thinkers have taken full advantage of Siddhartha's invitation to analyze his findings. Hundreds of books scrutinizing and debating his words are evidence of that. In fact, if you are interested in Buddhism, far from the threat of being labeled a blasphemer, you are encouraged to explore every doubt. Countless intelligent people have come to respect Siddhartha's wisdom and vision first. Only then do they offer their trust and devotion. It is for this reason that, once upon a time, princes and ministers didn't give a second thought to abandoning their palaces in the quest for truth.

PRACTICING HARMONY

Profound truths aside, these days even the most practical and obvious truths are ignored. We are like monkeys who dwell in the forest and shit on the very branches from which we hang. Every day we hear people talking about the state of the economy, not recognizing the connection between recession and greed.

Because of greed, jealousy, and pride, the economy will never become strong enough to ensure that every person has access to the basic necessities of life. Our dwelling place, the Earth, becomes more and more polluted. I have met people who condemn ancient rulers and emperors and ancient religions as the source of all conflict. But the secular and modern world has not done any better; if anything, it has done worse. What is it that the modern world has made better? One of the main effects of science and technology has been to destroy the world more quickly. Many scientists believe that all living systems and all life support systems on earth are in decline.

It's time for modern people like ourselves to give some thought to spiritual matters, even if we have no time to sit on a cushion, even if we are put off by those who wear rosaries around their necks, and even if we are embarrassed to exhibit our religious leanings to our secular friends. Contemplating the impermanent nature of everything that we experience and the painful effect of clinging to the self brings peace and harmony—if not to the entire world, at least within your own sphere.

As long as you accept and practice these four truths, you are a "practicing Buddhist." You might read about these four truths for the sake of entertainment or mental exercise, but if you don't practice them, you are like a sick person reading the label on a medicine bottle but never taking the medicine. On the other hand, if you are practicing, there is no need to exhibit that you are Buddhist. As a matter of fact, if it helps you to get invited to some social functions, it is totally fine to hide that you are a Buddhist. But keep in mind that as a Buddhist, you have a mission to refrain as much as possible from harming others, and to help others as much as possible. This is not a huge responsibility, because if you genuinely accept and contemplate the truths, all these deeds flow naturally.

It's also important to understand that as a Buddhist you do not have a mission or duty to convert the rest of the world to Buddhism. Buddhists and Buddhism are two different thing, like Democrats and democracy. I'm sure that many Buddhists have done and are doing awful things to themselves and others. But it is encouraging that until now Buddhists have not waged war or ransacked the temples of other religions in the name of the Buddha for the purpose of religious proselytizing.

As a Buddhist, you should stick with this policy: A Buddhist should never engage in or encourage bloodshed in the name of Buddhism. You cannot kill so much as one insect, let alone a human being. And if you happen to learn of an individual Buddhist or a group that is doing so, then as a Buddhist you must protest and condemn them. If you keep silent, you are not only not discouraging them, you are basically one of them. You are not a Buddhist.

Postscript on the Translation of Terms

I *have attempted to present the four views, the core of* Buddhist philosophy, in day-to-day language accessible to people from all walks of life. In doing so, I have had to make tough decisions regarding the choice of terminology. I think it is important to keep in mind that there is no real final consensus on the English translations for Sanskrit and Tibetan dharma terms. Within the different Buddhist schools, and even within a single Tibetan Buddhist school, there are variations in meaning and spelling. One good example is *zag bcas* (pronounced "zagchey") which we have translated here as "emotion," as in "all emotions are pain." That choice has raised eyebrows among those who think it is "too pervasive." Many people think not *all* emotions are pain. Yet it also raises the eyebrows of those who think it is not pervasive enough because the more precise translation of zag bcas is quite vast.

As Chokyi Nyima Rinpoche explains in his book *Indisputable Truth*, "The word zag bcas literally means 'involved in falling or shifting.'" He goes on to say:

> I once had the chance to ask Kunu Rinpoche, Tendzin Gyaltsen, about the meaning of this and some other Buddhist terms. He explained first the meaning of *person*, or *gangzag*, which contains one of the syllables in the word *defiling*. *Gang* means "any" or "whichever" in the sense of any

possible world or place of rebirth within the six classes of beings, while *zagpa* means "to fall into" or "shift" to one of those places. Thus, the word for *person* means "liable to transmigrate." He also mentioned that there is a traditional discussion about this etymology, since an arhat is also called a gangzag, personage.

Walpola Rahula, the author of *What the Buddha Taught*, translated the first seal as "All conditioned things are *dukkha* (suffering)." Others have used "All defiled or corrupted phenomena have the nature of the three sufferings." The Rangjung Yeshe dictionary gives a similar translation: "Everything that deteriorates is suffering."

One can still argue that all these translations are either too pervasive or not pervasive enough. To understand many of these terms, serious students will require further study and explanation. Fundamentally, anything that is subject to interdependence doesn't have sovereignty; it cannot fully control itself; and this dependence creates uncertainty, which is one of the main components of the Buddhist definition of "suffering." Therefore use of the English word *suffering* requires a lot of explanation.

Yet I have still decided to use the translation "All emotions are pain" so that readers will not look for the cause of their suffering externally. It makes it more personal—it's our mind and emotions.

Another thing readers should note is that the four seals as presented in this book are very Mahayana-oriented. Shravakayana traditions, such as Theravada, may not have these four seals; instead they may have only three. Those three are here in the four. Because this book is intended as a general presentation, I have decided that it is better to give more than less, all instead of just a few, and then there is no need to give more later.

ACKNOWLEDGMENTS

Speaking of compounded phenomena, I'd like to say that one does not have to look elsewhere for a good example. This book is a perfect example of compounded phenomena. Although some of the examples may be modern, the basic logic and premise of the arguments and analogies are something that has been taught. I've decided I don't need to be ashamed of plagiarizing the original ideas and teachings of the Buddha and many of his ancient followers, and especially of masters such as the great Guru Rinpoche Padmasambhava, Longchenpa, Milarepa, Gampopa, Sakya Pandita, Rigzin Jigme Lingpa, and Patrul Rinpoche. Those who have found a little bit of inspiration should therefore put some effort into getting to know some of these masters' work. I must here mention that if there are any grave mistakes or errors, either in words or in meaning, they are entirely my own doing, and while comments are very welcome, I would suggest it is a waste of your precious time.

The fact that it is at least readable is due to Noa Jones's effort, not only in terms of editing but also because she volunteered to be the "new to Buddhist philosophy" guinea pig. So my big appreciation and gratitude goes to her. Also I must acknowledge Jessie Wood, with her eagle eye for punctuation. And I must also thank all my friends—teenagers, scholars, beer-bellies, and thinkers—for bringing forth very challenging arguments that have helped shape this book. This book was conceived in a very funky cafe in Ubud, Bali, once a splendid Hindu kingdom; came into form amid the fog and cedar woods on the banks of Daisy Lake; and was completed in the Himalayas. May it bring some curiosity.

Dzongsar Khyentse has pledged his profits from this book to the Khyentse Foundation, a nonprofit organization founded in 2001 to support institutions and individuals engaged in the practice and study of Buddha's vision of wisdom and compassion. The foundation carries out this mission by means of a number of projects including, but not limited to, a scholarship fund, an endowment for monastic education, a publications fund, endowments to promote Buddhist studies at major universities, and Buddhist schools for children. More information can be found at www.khyentsefoundation.org.

KHYENTSE
FOUNDATION